The History of Palestine

Exploring the Past and Present of a Contested Land

Written by Matthew Rivers

The History of Palestine

*Exploring the Past and Present
of a Contested Land*

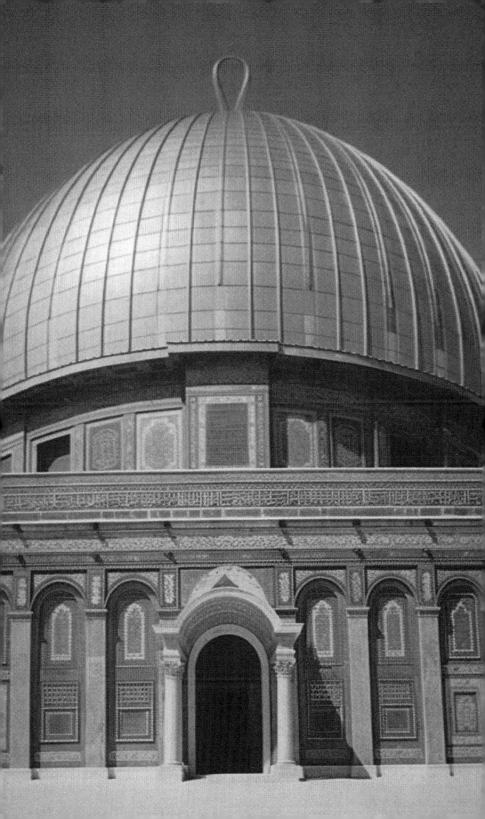

Contents

A Note From the Author

Thank you for embarking on this journey into the history of Palestine, a place that has served as an epicenter of civilization, spirituality, and conflict for millennia. The pages of this book carry within them the stories, lives, triumphs, and tragedies that have made Palestine what it is today - a tapestry of cultures, religions, and identities that bear testament to a history as rich as it is complex.

The task of compiling the history of a place that has been revered, fought over, celebrated, and mourned in equal measure was indeed a daunting one. Every stone in its ancient cities, every verse in its sacred texts, every artifact unearthed from its storied ground has a tale to tell. It has been my endeavor to do justice to these tales, ensuring that every epoch, from the earliest civilizations to modern times, has been examined with the care, precision, and empathy it deserves.

This book offers an exploration into the varied epochs that have shaped Palestine, starting from the prehistoric era and continuing through the Bronze and Iron Ages. It delves into the impacts of Canaanite, Philistine, and Israelite influences, followed by the changes brought about by Babylonian, Persian, Hellenistic, and Roman rule. As we move forward in time, we delve into the Byzantine era, the coming of the Islamic caliphates, and the turbulence of the Crusades.

The more recent past is not overlooked, with extensive chapters on the periods of Mamluk and Ottoman rule, the consequential effects of World War I, and the ensuing British Mandate period. The book closely examines the Balfour Declaration, Zionist immigration, Arab revolts, and the United Nations Partition Plan.

The book delves into the Suez Crisis, the Six-Day War, the Yom Kippur War, and the expansion of Israel's borders. It also analyzes the Intifadas, the peace processes, and the intricate political and social struggles that have ensued. We probe into the roles of various international organizations, the divisions between Fatah and Hamas, the enduring status of Jerusalem, and the living conditions in the Occupied Territories.

The History of Palestine, while being a comprehensive exploration, is also a humane inquiry. It seeks not just to recount the political and social changes, but also to remember the people who lived these histories, their joys and sorrows, their hopes and dreams, their losses and victories. As you journey through these pages, my hope is that you gain an understanding that transcends mere historical facts and enters into the heart of what makes Palestine such a significant place in our shared global heritage.

I extend my gratitude to you, dear reader, for taking this journey with me. Whether you are a student of history, an observer of current events, or someone seeking a deeper understanding of this region that holds such a significant place in our global consciousness, I hope this book will serve as a guide, a resource, and, ultimately, a bridge towards a better understanding.

Best regards,

Matthew Rivers

Prehistoric Palestine

The land now known as Palestine has a long and storied history, stretching back to the earliest days of human civilization. Nestled in the eastern Mediterranean, this narrow strip of territory has seen the rise and fall of empires, the birth and spread of new religions, and countless struggles for power and control. Its unique geographic location – at the crossroads of Europe, Asia, and Africa – has made it a battleground for competing interests and a fertile ground for the exchange of ideas and cultures. As we trace the development of Palestine through the ages, we cannot help but marvel at the resilience of its people and the incredible role this small region has played in shaping the broader currents of world history.

Our journey begins in the dimly-lit caverns of the prehistoric era, a time when early humans roamed the verdant landscapes of the Levant. We will explore the lives of these early inhabitants, a motley collective of hunters, gatherers, and wandering tribes, who first left their indelible mark upon the land. Unearthing the secrets of the Paleolithic era, we will see how these simple people wrested a living from the earth and crafted tools from flint and bone, not knowing that their earliest innovations would echo throughout the long corridors of history.

In time, these scattered, nomadic groups would coalesce into more sophisticated societies, laying the foundations for the impressive city-states that will emerge in the Bronze Age. This crucial turning point in Palestine's history sees the rise of powerful kingdoms, expansive trade networks, and advancements in agriculture, technology, and warfare. As we delve into the developments of the Bronze Age, we will encounter rival empires vying for control, fortified cities standing against the march of time, and the emergence of common languages, religious beliefs, and cultural practices that bind these disparate peoples together.

The onset of the Iron Age transforms the landscape of prehistoric Palestine into a rich tapestry of competing kingdoms, each seeking to carve out a niche in a world defined by scarcity and conflict. In this volatile era, the names of ancient cities such as Jerusalem, Megiddo, and Ashkelon will be etched into the annals of history – their stories of struggle, perseverance, and triumph captured in the words and deeds of their rulers, priests, and everyday citizens. As we explore this tumultuous epoch, we will seek to understand the complex interplay of forces that animate these societies, giving voice to the people who shaped the destiny of their lands through diplomacy, warfare, and the power of the written word.

Paleolithic Era

The earliest human remains in the region of Palestine were found in Ubeidiya, located south of the Sea of Galilee in the Jordan Rift Valley. Dated to the Pleistocene epoch around 1.5 million years ago, these remains provide traces of the earliest migration of Homo erectus out of Africa. The hand axes discovered at this site have been identified as Acheulean, a widely recognized hallmark of the era.

Another significant site in understanding early human migration to Palestine is Nahal Amud, where the first prehistoric dig in Palestine was conducted. The discovery of the "Galilee Skull" in the nearby Zuttiyeh Cave in 1925 offered further clues into human development within the area. Qafzeh, an important paleoanthropological site south of Nazareth, has provided valuable information about our direct Homo sapiens ancestors. Eleven significant, fossilized Homo sapiens skeletons were discovered within the main rock shelter. These modern human remains, including both adults and infants, are dated to approximately 90,000 to 100,000 years ago. Interestingly, many of the bones found at Qafzeh were stained with red ochre, suggesting its use in burial rituals and pointing toward the emergence of symbolic thought and intelligence in early human populations.

Palestine's Mount Carmel region has revealed a number of important findings, particularly from the Kebara Cave, which was inhabited between 60,000 and 48,000 years ago, and where the most complete Neanderthal skeleton has been found to date. The Tabun Cave in the same vicinity displays evidence of intermittent occupation during both the Lower and Middle Paleolithic eras, ranging from 500,000 to around 40,000 years ago. Excavations at the site suggest one of the longest sequences of human occupation in the Levant.

Another noteworthy discovery comes from Skhul Cave, near Mount Carmel, where evidence of the late Epipalaeolithic Natufian culture was found. This culture is characterized by the presence of abundant microliths, human burials, and ground stone tools. This site also presents a unique example of Neanderthals and modern humans living side by side. Neanderthals were present in the region from 200,000 to 45,000 years ago, with modern humans dating back to 100,000 years ago.

In the caves of Shuqba in Ramallah and Wadi Khareitun in Bethlehem, artifacts such as stone, wood, and animal bone tools attributed to the Natufian culture (c. 12,800-10,300 BCE) were uncovered. Additional remains associated with this era have been discovered at sites such as Tel Abu Hureura, Ein Mallaha, Beidha, and Jericho.

The evolution of early human societies from hunter-gatherers to agricultural communities took place between 10,000 and 5,000 BCE. Evidence of such settlements can be observed at Tel es-Sultan in Jericho, where walls, a religious shrine, and a 23-foot (7.0 m) tower with an internal staircase have been discovered. Jericho itself is believed to be one of the oldest continuously inhabited cities in the world, with evidence of settlement dating back to 9,000 BCE. This site provides critical information about the early human communities in the Near East.

As human societies continued to grow and develop during this period, migration along the Jericho-Dead Sea-Bir es-Saba-Gaza-Sinai route brought new groups and cultures to the region, which in turn contributed to the increasing urban landscape. These migrants used copper and stone tools, signaling advancements in technology and cultural exchange.

The Paleolithic era in Palestine tells an engrossing tale of the ebb and flow of early human migration, occupation, and development in the region. This period stood witness to the evolution of early Homo sapiens, a species which would eventually dominate the world. Alongside these burgeoning Homo sapiens, the Neanderthals also inhabited the region, an interspecies coexistence that lends a fascinating dimension to the history of human evolution. The emergence of symbolic thought, rituals, and tool usage were remarkable hallmarks of this era, underscoring the beginning of a cognitive revolution and the dawn of culture. The ongoing debate regarding the relationships, interactions, and possibly interbreeding between Neanderthals and modern humans only adds to the richness and complexity of the prehistoric history of Palestine. This era, teeming with evolutionary leaps and burgeoning cognitive prowess, laid the groundwork for the civilization that was to come.

Bronze Age Developments

As time rolled on, the world entered the Bronze Age, a period marked by significant developments and eventual upheaval. The late Bronze Age, in particular, heralded a time of profound changes that would shape the Ancient Near East, including the region of Canaan, for centuries to follow. The most impactful of these developments was the abrupt withdrawal of the Egyptians from the region. Their departure marked the end of an epoch, where for centuries Egyptian power had directly and indirectly cast a long shadow over the Near East. This withdrawal wasn't an overnight event but rather a gradual receding tide that left a power vacuum in its wake. The reasons behind this retreat are a subject of constant scholarly debate, with theories ranging from economic downturns to climatic changes. Regardless of the cause, the consequences of this withdrawal were unequivocal, serving as the catalyst for a seismic shift in the regional power balance. It formed the bedrock for a multitude of significant changes, a period of flux that gave rise to new power structures and civilizational shifts in this cradle of early human development.

Archaeological investigations have discovered layers of destruction from this crisis period across numerous sites, such as Hazor, Beit She'an, Megiddo, Lachish, Ekron, Ashdod, and Ashkelon. It is important to note that these destruction layers are not uniform in their dating. For instance, the destruction of Lachish and Megiddo can be dated back to around 1130 BCE, over a century after the destruction of Hazor in approximately 1250 BCE. This evidence suggests that the decline was far from sudden and uniform, but rather a prolonged process that played out over many decades.

As the Egyptian influence waned during the late 13th century, Canaan witnessed a surge in the establishment of smaller, unprotected village settlements. Many of these settlements were founded in the mountainous regions, possibly signifying attempts by the inhabitants to take refuge in more defensible positions. In some of the settlements, the architectural characteristics commonly associated with the later inhabitants of Israel and Judah start to emerge, such as the quintessential four-room house.

However, the number of these smaller village settlements began to decline in the 11th century. This reduction in village numbers was offset by other settlements that transitioned and expanded to become fortified townships. These fortified settlements provided improved security and defense capabilities for their inhabitants, indicating a shift in priorities and the emergence of more organized socio-political units. The fortified townships signaled a movement towards urbanization, concentrating resources and power in fewer, more secure locations.

The transition towards fortified settlements during this time raises intriguing questions about the underlying causes and effects of the changes in the broader socio-political landscape. The prolonged decline in local civilization might have been fueled by a combination of economic, political, and environmental factors. These factors could have created an atmosphere of insecurity and competition, driving the rise of new power centers and alliances to counteract the lack of centralized authority.

The Late Bronze Age developments provide valuable insights into the formation of new political entities and the resilient nature of the inhabitants of the region. As Egypt's authority and protection waned, social and political reorganization was necessary to adapt to the evolving circumstances. The fortified townships and distinct architectural styles that emerged during this period can be seen as a precursor to later Israelite and Judean cultures and their determination to seek protection and independence in a tumultuous world.

The Bronze Age developments in Prehistoric Palestine illuminate how this region adapted and restructured in response to a major historical crisis. While the collapse marked the end of many ancient empires, it also laid the groundwork for the emergence of new societies and political systems that would continue to shape the region well into the future.

Iron Age Onset

As the sun set on the Late Bronze Age, a new dawn broke over the eastern Mediterranean, heralding an era of profound transformation – the Iron Age. This period of transition, marked by the widespread adoption of iron metallurgy, also bore witness to sweeping geopolitical, societal, and cultural shifts. Among these changes was the sudden fragmentation of the region, a consequence of the spectacular collapse of the Bronze Age superpowers, notably the Hittite Empire and Egyptian control in Canaan.

The region's power vacuum became a catalyst for change, opening doors for new cultural groups to gain prominence. Among them were various tribes in Palestine, which, while not initially successful in establishing a foothold, gradually became more permanent fixtures in the region by the 12th century BCE. The Israelite tribes were one such group. Their history, a tapestry woven from archaeological evidence and ancient textual narratives, including the Hebrew Bible, suggests they descended from a patriarch named Israel or Jacob. However, the precise origins of the Israelites remain a matter of scholarly debate, with theories ranging from an external arrival to an internal emergence from the local Canaanite population.

As the Late Bronze Age gradually transitioned into the Iron Age, the evolving landscape of the region witnessed the rise of a potent force that would greatly influence its historical trajectory: the Sea Peoples. These maritime marauders, shrouded in the mists of history, posed a formidable threat to the established kingdoms of the era.

Their origins, a mystery that continues to baffle historians, range from the islands of the Aegean Sea to the coasts of Western Anatolia and even Southern Europe.

The Sea Peoples, known primarily from ancient Egyptian records, embarked on a series of aggressive seaborne invasions, sowing chaos and destruction across Egypt and other parts of the Eastern Mediterranean. Their impact was both immediate and far-reaching, triggering a cascade of destabilization across the established geopolitical order. Kingdoms fell and trade networks collapsed, marking a significant rupture in the Bronze Age world and hastening the advent of the Iron Age.

These invasions are particularly notable for the relentless pressure they applied to the dominant powers of the day. The powerful Hittite Empire crumbled, and Egypt, although managing to fend off the Sea Peoples, suffered severe economic and political strains. The scale and intensity of these disruptions signified a major turning point, a period of significant turmoil and change.

In the context of Palestine, the reverberations from these distant upheavals offered unexpected advantages for the Israelite tribes that were beginning to make their mark in the region. The marauding Sea Peoples' invasions significantly weakened the Canaanite city-states, which had been dominant in Palestine during the Late Bronze Age. With these city-states in disarray, they were unable to assert control over the dispersed Israelite clans scattered across the region.

This indirect protection offered by the chaos induced by the Sea Peoples had a profound impact on the Israelites.

It provided them with a strategic window of opportunity to consolidate their position, unhindered by the resurgent Canaanite powers. Moreover, it allowed them to extend their influence and control across the region, setting the stage for their eventual formation into a unified kingdom under figures like King David and King Solomon.

Among the Sea Peoples, one group, the Philistines or the Peleset, settled along the southern coastal plain of Canaan, creating a powerful cultural and political entity that would often clash with the Israelite tribes. Their presence further diversified the socio-political landscape of the region during the Iron Age.

In essence, the Sea Peoples, through their invasive actions, became inadvertent architects of a new era, their disruptions creating a domino effect that reshaped the political and cultural map of the Eastern Mediterranean.

Canaanites, Philistines, and Israelites

In the sun-scorched lands of ancient Palestine, a drama was unfolding that would shape the destinies of nations, influence modern global politics, and leave an indelible mark on the history of human civilization. At the crossroads of Africa, Asia, and Europe, three distinct groups – the Canaanites, the Philistines, and the Israelites – were embroiled in a complex and often deadly struggle for power, territory, identity, and beliefs. This rich and diverse corner of the ancient world witnessed the rise and fall of civilizations, the birth of great empires, and the establishment of enduring religious traditions that would resonate for millennia.

The sophisticated Canaanite civilization, with its thriving cities, grand temples, and far-reaching trade networks, was the forerunner of all that would follow. As we delve into the mysteries of their culture, we shall bear witness to the rise and decline of a great society that laid much of the groundwork for the region's future development. The world owes a great deal to these ancient pioneers, as many aspects of modern society have been influenced by their achievements and innovations, both in the arts and sciences.

Next, we shall meet the enigmatic Philistines, a people who arrived from the sea and settled on the coastal plains of Palestine. Though often depicted as marauders, these seafaring peoples brought with them an advanced material culture which included valuable skills in metallurgy and an impressive array of artistic crafts, leaving a lasting impact on the region. Emerging as neighbors and later rivals to the Israelites, their relationship was anything but cordial and their conflict would shape much of the region's history.

The Israelites, a seminomadic group who were united under a shared belief system, gradually became a prominent force in the region. With fascinating figures such as King David and King Solomon at their helm, they expanded their territory and influence, while establishing a lasting spiritual legacy through their beliefs and traditions. The building of Solomon's Temple in Jerusalem, a monumental achievement of ancient architecture and a symbol of Israelite success, would have reverberations that still persist in the world of today.

As we traverse this intriguing landscape, it is important to recognize that the destinies of the Canaanites, Philistines, and Israelites were inextricably linked – intertwined by trade, war, cultural exchange, and religious upheaval. We shall unveil the stories behind these ancient peoples – their successes, their failures, and ultimately, their legacies. By understanding their struggles, we can better appreciate the foundations upon which many aspects of our own world have been built.

Canaanite Civilization

Canaan, a civilization that flourished in the southern Levant during the late 2nd millennium BC, bore a significant geopolitical influence during the period. Located at the intersection of the spheres of interest of major empires including the Egyptians, Hittites, Mitanni, and Assyrians, the region held strategic importance due to its location and resources. Its prominence and influence are demonstrated through archaeological excavations carried out in crucial areas like Tel Hazor, Tel Megiddo, En Esur, and Gezer, which provide a detailed account of the civilization's rich history and cultural diversity.

The name "Canaan" not only features frequently in the Bible but holds significant relevance, often associated with the "Promised Land." This term, "Promised Land," originates from the promises made by God to Abraham and his descendants in the Book of Genesis. Specifically, in Genesis 12:7, 15:18, and 17:8, God promises to give the land of Canaan to Abraham's descendants as an everlasting possession, establishing an eternal covenant with them.

In the biblical narrative, Canaan represents a land of abundance and prosperity, a place where "milk and honey flow." It's often depicted as a symbol of divine favor and reward, embodying the promises of God to His chosen people. Canaan's association with the concept of a "Promised Land" speaks to its cultural and religious significance, not only to the Israelites but to all of Christianity and Judaism.

Contrary to popular belief, Canaanite culture wasn't homogenous but rather a rich tapestry of cultural influences, reflecting the diversity of populations in the area. This is evidenced by the extensive archaeological findings from different regions, each bearing its unique cultural footprint.

Prominent biblical scholar Mark Smith highlighted the substantial overlap between Canaanite and Israelite cultures. According to Smith, Israelite culture not only coexisted with Canaanite culture but also significantly derived from it. This fact presents a thought-provoking perspective on the Canaanites, depicting them as the cultural progenitors of one of history's most influential civilizations.

Around 500 BC, the people identified as Canaanites were known to the Ancient Greeks as Phoenicians, indicating the continued influence of the Canaanite civilization into the 1st millennium BC. The name "Canaanites" also survived through the Punics, a group of Canaanite-speakers who emigrated to Carthage in the 9th century BC. During Late Antiquity, the Punics of North Africa continued to identify themselves as "Chanani," preserving the legacy of Canaanite civilization long after its decline.

Philistine Arrival and Influence

The Philistines were an ancient people who lived on the south coast of Canaan during the Iron Age. Originating from the Aegean, they arrived in Canaan around 1175 BCE and gradually assimilated into the Levantine societies while preserving their unique culture. Over time, the Philistines developed a distinct material culture that has come to define their existence.

The Hebrew Bible is the primary source of information about the Philistines, detailing their frequent clashes with the Israelites. However, other archaeological sources also provide vital insight into their history. One such source is the Temple of Ramses III at Medinet Habu, which features Philistines depicted as Peleset, a term believed to be cognate with the Hebrew Peleshet. Assyrian records similarly provide parallel terms for the Philistines, such as Palastu, Pilišti, and Pilistu.

Throughout their time in Canaan, the Philistines maintained a tenuous relationship with the Israelites, as documented in the Hebrew Bible. This conflict was driven by disputes over territory and resources as both groups sought to establish themselves in the region. The biblical narrative is filled with stories of famous battles between the two, such as the story of David and Goliath, showcasing the long-standing animosity between the Philistines and the Israelites.

The cultural influence of the Philistines can be observed through their contributions to art, architecture, and other areas of society. Their distinct material culture, which developed as a result of their arrival in Canaan, has allowed archaeologists and historians to better understand the nature of their interactions with other groups in the region. The Philistines' artistic influence has been observed in pottery styles, sculptures, and decorative features of their cities.

In terms of socio-political dynamics, the Philistine presence in Canaan was marked by complex interactions with neighboring groups, including the Israelites, Canaanites, and later the Assyrians and Babylonians. As an immigrant group, the Philistines initially struggled for control of the region but eventually forged a place for themselves in the Levantine political landscape. Ultimately, however, the Philistine polity was subjugated by the Neo-Assyrian Empire before being destroyed by King Nebuchadnezzar II of the Neo-Babylonian Empire in 604 BCE. Their incorporation into these larger empires led to their loss of distinct ethnic identity, and they disappeared from the historical and archaeological records by the late 5th century BCE.

The arrival and influence of the Philistines significantly impacted the cultural, social, and political fabric of ancient Palestine. Their interaction with the Israelites and other neighboring groups shaped the course of regional history. By examining the Philistines' role in ancient Palestine, we are not only able to gain insight into the broader historical narrative but also better contextualize their actions and assess the true measure of their influence on the region.

Rise of the Israelite Kingdom

During the 10th and 9th centuries BCE, a significant shift occurred in the geopolitical landscape of the ancient Near East, leading to the emergence of two distinct but related Israelite kingdoms - Israel in the north and Judah in the south. The division between these two kingdoms can be traced back to complex socio-political and religious factors that evolved over time.

The establishment of these two kingdoms is intrinsically linked to the narrative of the Twelve Tribes of Israel, as described in the Bible. According to biblical tradition, the Twelve Tribes were named after the twelve sons of Jacob, also known as Israel. Over time, these tribes settled in different regions of Canaan and developed distinct political, social, and religious practices.

The united monarchy under Kings Saul, David, and Solomon, which supposedly lasted from about 1020 to 930 BCE, is believed to have split into two after Solomon's death. This split is often attributed to economic and administrative burdens of Solomon's ambitious building programs and military campaigns, leading to public discontent and ultimately civil war. As a result, ten of the northern tribes rebelled and formed the independent Kingdom of Israel, leaving the tribes of Judah and Benjamin in the south as the Kingdom of Judah.

Israel, often referred to as the Northern Kingdom, was the larger and more prosperous of the two, developing into a regional power. This prosperity can be attributed to its fertile land and strategic location on important trade routes connecting Egypt and Mesopotamia. However, this also meant that it was frequently threatened by powerful neighboring empires.

By the 8th century BCE, the Israelite population had significantly increased, reaching approximately 160,000 individuals across 500 settlements. This growth can be attributed to various factors, including the region's natural fertility, advances in agricultural practices, and possibly an influx of people from surrounding areas, seeking the relative stability and prosperity that the Israelite kingdoms offered.

During this period, the Kingdoms of Israel and Judah found themselves in regular conflict with the neighboring kingdoms of Ammon, Edom, and Moab, located in what is now Jordan, as well as with the Kingdom of Aram-Damascus, situated in modern-day Syria. These conflicts were often about territorial control and access to vital trade routes.

Despite the political divisions that characterized the Israelite kingdoms of Israel and Judah, a significant unifying factor remained - the flourishing of Hebrew as both a spoken and written language.

The use of Hebrew language became one of the core aspects of the Israelite identity during this period. It was not merely a tool for communication, but also a critical vehicle for cultural expression, religious observance, and legal proceedings, playing a central role in the daily lives of the people and their collective consciousness.

Hebrew emerged from the Canaanite language family around the 12th century BCE, but it was during the period of the Israelite kingdoms, particularly between the 10th and 7th centuries BCE, that it truly blossomed and expanded. It was used widely in various contexts - from administrative record-keeping and legal documentation to literary creativity and religious scripture. This period saw the production of some of the most significant Hebrew texts, including large portions of what would later be compiled into the Hebrew Bible.

Hebrew script evolved during this period, transitioning from the early Phoenician script to the Paleo-Hebrew script, a writing system that was distinctively Israelite. This script was used for both secular and religious texts, including royal inscriptions, legal codes, and the early versions of biblical texts.

Despite the geopolitical challenges and threats that the Israelite kingdoms faced, the continuity of the Hebrew language and its evolution as a sophisticated tool for written communication served to unite the people, preserving their collective identity and cultural heritage. This linguistic unity allowed the Israelite culture to thrive, even amidst political turmoil, reinforcing shared traditions and values that would continue to define the Israelite and later Jewish identity for centuries to come.

Babylonian, Persian, and Hellenistic Rule

Throughout the course of history, the world has witnessed the rise and fall of several great empires, and it was from these events that societies could chart new paths, forge new alliances, and find themselves transformed by new avenues of thought, culture, and religion. One such pivotal era in human history unraveled in the Levant region more than two millennia ago, as three successive world powers – the Babylonians, Persians, and Hellenistic empires – exerted their influence over the Jewish people, and as a result, shaped the history of Western civilization as we know it today.

To fully understand the complexity and nuances of the intrigues played out in ancient Near East, this chapter will delve deep into the intricacies of the events that unfolded during these fascinating times, and examine the personalities, momentous battles, and intricate politics that shaped the world back then. We shall embark on a journey to explore the tragic Babylonian exile and the destruction of the First Temple - events that forever changed the lives of an entire nation and altered the course of their history.

As our story continues, we will see how the tides of fortune shifted under Persian rule, enabling the Jewish people to re-establish their homeland, rebuild their sacred temple, and attempt to forge a new identity, all while navigating the complexities of hegemonic power. The narrative will delve into the delicate diplomatic maneuvers and brave resilience demonstrated by the exiles under the reign of the Achaemenid Empire.

As the story unfolds, we enter the vibrant and chaotic world of Hellenistic influence, where cultures collided, and the Jewish people found themselves caught in a tumultuous struggle between the allure of Greek civilization and the preservation of their own identity. We will shed light on the bitter conflict that ensued, pitting brother against brother, and the fight for religious and political control that swept through their lands.

In a rousing turn of events, the Maccabean revolt will take center stage, illustrating the enduring human spirit's fight for freedom and the face of seemingly insurmountable odds. We will follow the valiant Judah Maccabee and his dedicated followers as they embark on their quest to defend their faith against the oppressive forces of Antiochus IV Epiphanes.

Last, but by no means least, the narrative will culminate in the rise of the Hasmonean Dynasty. We will explore the ascendancy of the Maccabean leaders and the establishment of an independent Jewish state, only for it to be riddled with family strife and political scheming that ultimately sealed its fate.

The course of history is often shaped by the most unexpected twists, and the lessons it teaches us continue to reverberate today. Thus, it is imperative to explore the threads of history and connect the dots to understand our own place in the grand tapestry of time. The events that transpired during the Babylonian, Persian, and Hellenistic eras have laid the groundwork for contemporary politics, religion, and society, making it an essential historical period for all to study. As we journey through tales of triumph, tragedy, and transformation, may the stories of the past provide insights that enable us to be more conscientious connoisseurs of our present reality.

Babylonian Exile and Destruction of the First Temple

The power struggles and the eventual decline of the Assyrian Empire in the 7th century BCE allowed for the rise of Babylon and its conquest of most of Assyria's territories. Amid the conflict between Babylon and Egypt for dominance over the region, the Kingdom of Judah was caught in the middle. Despite the warnings of the prophet Jeremiah, the Kingdom of Judah sought an alliance with Egypt, attempting to secure protection from the Babylonian threat.

However, the Babylonian king Nebuchadnezzar seized the opportunity to invade Judah in response to their defection, laying siege to Jerusalem in 598 BCE. This led to the deportation of King Jeconiah, Jerusalem's elite class, and its priesthood to Babylon.

During the 10th Century BCE, Solomon, the penultimate ruler of the United Kingdom of Israel, is believed to have commissioned the construction of the First Temple in Jerusalem. Based on narratives in the Hebrew Bible, the temple served as a religious center, a place for worship, and a place of assembly for the Israelites.

The descriptions of the First Temple are largely derived from the Hebrew Bible, specifically the Book of Kings. It is believed that Solomon placed the Ark of the Covenant, a symbol of Israel's God, in the Holy of Holies, a windowless inner sanctum within the temple. This sacred chamber was off-limits to most people, with only the High Priest of Israel allowed entry on Yom Kippur, carrying the blood of a sacrificial lamb and burning incense.

The First Temple, or Solomon's Temple as it is often called, played a pivotal role in the spiritual life of the Israelites during the First Temple period (c. 957-587 BCE). It was much more than a physical edifice; it was the central place of worship, a tangible symbol of the Israelites' covenant with their God, Yahweh.

Prior to the First Temple, the religious practices of the Israelites, as reflected in archaeological findings and biblical accounts, appear to have been diverse and often incorporated elements of polytheism or monolatrism. Monolatrism is a type of polytheism where one deity is worshipped, but the existence of other deities is recognized. In the case of the Israelites, this took the form of Yahwism, where Yahweh was worshipped above all others, but other gods and goddesses were not necessarily denied. Canaanite deities like Baal, Asherah, and others seemed to have had some presence in Israelite religious practice. There are numerous biblical references to the Israelites falling into the worship of these "foreign" gods, suggesting a tension between the monotheistic worship of Yahweh and the polytheistic practices prevalent in the region.

However, the destruction of the First Temple in 587 BCE by King Nebuchadnezzar II of the Neo-Babylonian Empire marked a seismic shift in the religious landscape of the Israelites. The subsequent Babylonian captivity, where much of the Jewish population was exiled to Babylon, was seen as a divine punishment for the people's failure to uphold their covenant with Yahweh. This period of exile was a time of profound reflection and transformation for the Jewish faith.

Amid the violence and devastation, ancient accounts describe a moment at the destruction of the Temple when an enraged Babylonian officer, Nebuzaradan, discovered the still-seething blood of the martyred prophet Zechariah. Compelled to appease the restless spirit of Zechariah, Nebuzaradan carried out a massacre, killing 940,000 people in the city before the blood finally receded.

This tragic destruction of Jerusalem and the First Temple marked the end of David and Solomon's empire, fulfilling the warnings issued by Moses in the Torah. Jeremiah, on the other hand, had also prophesied the eventual return of the Jewish people to Jerusalem and the rebuilding of the Temple, a promise that would materialize seventy years later. The period of the Babylonian exile was a turning point in the history of the Jewish people, who, amidst the devastation and loss, would eventually redefine and reshape their identity and faith as they emerged from the ashes.

The catastrophic loss of the Temple and the homeland was interpreted by many as the fulfillment of biblical prophecies warning of such a calamity as retribution for abandoning monotheistic worship. This narrative fueled a shift in religious perspective and practice towards a more rigorous monotheism. During the Babylonian exile, the Israelites began to view Yahweh not just as their tribal god or the highest god in a pantheon, but as the only God, rejecting the worship of other deities entirely.

The transformation from polytheism or monolatrism to a firm belief in Jewish monotheism during this period was a significant milestone in the history of Judaism. This theological shift was integral in shaping the religious identity of the Jewish people, influencing their liturgical practices, societal norms, and cultural expressions, and laying the groundwork for the development of monotheistic religions, including Christianity and Islam, in later centuries.

However, controversies and debates surround the construction of Solomon's Temple and its actual existence. Until the 1980s, many scholars accepted the biblical account of Solomon's Temple as authentic. However, skeptical approaches to the biblical text and the lack of archaeological evidence cast doubt on the existence of the temple as early as the 10th century BCE. Some scholars have posited that the original structure built by Solomon was quite modest and later rebuilt on a larger scale.

One of the challenges in confirming the existence of Solomon's Temple is the lack of direct archaeological evidence. No recent excavations have taken place in the Temple Mount area due to religious and political sensitivities, making it difficult to ascertain the temple's historical accuracy. Nineteenth and early-twentieth-century excavations in and around the Temple Mount did not yield any traces of the complex.

Nevertheless, some archaeological discoveries offer hints about the First Temple's existence. The House of Yahweh ostracon, dating back to the 6th century BCE, may refer to the temple. In the 21st century, two key findings have been discovered in present-day Israel bearing resemblance to the biblical description of Solomon's Temple. These include a shrine model from the early half of the 10th century BCE in Khirbet Qeiyafa and the Tel Motza temple, which dates back to the 9th century BCE and is located in the Motza neighborhood within West Jerusalem.

Persian Rule and Restoration

The transition of power to the Persian Achaemenid Empire, led by Cyrus the Great, heralded a significant shift in the history of the Near East. Cyrus's conquest of Babylon in 539 BCE is viewed as a pivotal moment that reshaped the geopolitical landscape of the region.

Prior to his conquest, Babylon, under the rule of the Neo-Babylonian Empire, held significant sway over much of the ancient Near East. However, the Neo-Babylonian Empire's dominance was short-lived. Their fall began when Cyrus, a Persian king from the region of Anshan, embarked on a series of ambitious military campaigns, gradually consolidating power and expanding the influence of the Persian Achaemenid Empire.

Cyrus's conquest of Babylon was notably documented in the Cyrus Cylinder, a remarkable artifact often referred to as the first charter of human rights. In it, Cyrus expressed his respect for the cultural, religious, and administrative traditions of Babylon, signaling a departure from the brutal domination tactics of previous empires.

After his conquest, Cyrus declared the liberation of the Jewish captives in Babylon, an act often linked to the concept of the "right of return" in Jewish history. This marked the end of the Babylonian captivity, a significant period in Jewish history when many Jews had been exiled to Babylon following the fall of the Kingdom of Judah.

Following the conquest, Cyrus's administration extended its control over the region of Palestine, establishing at least five provinces: Yehud Medinata, Samaria, Gaza, Ashdod, and Ascalon. The Persian administrative system was notably tolerant, allowing a degree of local autonomy and cultural diversity. This contributed to a period of relative stability and prosperity, with the Phoenician city-states, especially those in present-day Lebanon, flourishing, and Arabian tribes migrating to the southern deserts.

This transition marked a new epoch in the historical and cultural landscape of Palestine and the broader Near East, setting the stage for the cultural developments and geopolitical shifts that would define the region in the centuries to come.

In a significant departure from previous conquest strategies, Cyrus the Great issued a proclamation that granted religious freedom to subjugated populations. The Persian Empire allowed exiles to return to their homeland and rebuild their temples, a policy that earned them goodwill among the conquered populations. Consequently, in 538 BCE, the exiled Judeans were permitted to return to Jerusalem, where they became known as Jews and established Yehud Medinata, a self-governing Jewish province under Persian rule. Yehud Medinata witnessed the rebuilding of the First Temple, which the Babylonians had destroyed.

Major religious transformations occurred during this period as the Israelite religion continued to become exclusively monotheistic, with Yahweh as the sole god. Numerous customs and behaviors that characterize Judaism were adopted during this time. The region of Samaria was inhabited by the Samaritans, an ethnoreligious group who, like the Jews, worshipped Yahweh and claimed ancestry to the Israelites. The Samaritan temple cult on Mount Gerizim competed with the Jews' temple cult in Jerusalem, leading to enduring animosity between the two groups.

In Palestine, the Edomites were another significant group. Initially, their kingdom occupied present-day southern Jordan, but due to pressures from nomadic tribes, they migrated into southern parts of Judea and established Idumea. During this period, the Persians granted the Phoenician kings of Tyre and Sidon control over the coastal plain and the Upper Galilee, enabling them to dominate the entire coast up to Ascalon in the southern coastal plain.

Nomadic Arabian tribes in the Negev desert played a vital role in the Persian Empire because they controlled important trade routes. Despite facing some challenges, such as the Qedarites losing their trade privileges after a failed revolt, these tribes continued to impact the region significantly, with the Nabataeans later establishing a flourishing civilization in the Negev.

The intermingling of Persian and Greek cultures during the Persian rule of Palestine significantly impacted the region, ushering in a period of Hellenization that had far-reaching effects on the local society. Despite the ongoing Greco-Persian Wars, Greek cultural influences pervaded the area, brought by traders, artisans, and coins, which became an essential medium for cultural exchange.

Greek coins, for example, circulated widely, providing more than just a medium of economic exchange. The motifs, symbols, and depictions on these coins served as vehicles for disseminating Greek mythology, art styles, and beliefs. They effectively communicated the Greek worldview, subtly promoting Hellenistic values and norms among the local population.

Alongside monetary influence, Greek traders played a substantial role in increasing cultural interaction. Establishing trading posts along the coast, they brought a wide array of Greek goods, including luxury items such as pottery, jewelry, and wine. The popularity of these items grew among the local populace, who began to covet them as symbols of affluence and cultural refinement. Greek goods were not only highly sought after but also frequently imitated, testifying to the profound influence Greek culture exerted on local artisans and craftsmen.

Indeed, the local population's fascination with Greek culture manifested in various areas of life, from commerce to craft production. For instance, coinage minted in the province of Yehud during this period reflects the ongoing Hellenistic influence. Often, these local coins bore the symbols or iconography reminiscent of Greek designs, representing an intriguing blend of local and foreign cultural elements.

Moreover, the adoption of Greek cultural norms extended beyond material culture to encompass elements of language, literature, philosophy, and governance. The permeation of Greek influence into Palestinian society during this time laid the groundwork for the more extensive Hellenization that would occur following the conquests of Alexander the Great in the later fourth century BCE.

Despite political hostilities between the Greeks and Persians, the Greek cultural influence in Palestine during the Persian period was substantial. It marked a transformative phase in the region's cultural history, sowing the seeds of

Hellenistic culture in the fertile soils of the Near East.

Political struggles between Egypt and Persia caused fluctuations in territorial control, with both nations vying for influence in Palestine and Phoenicia. Although Egypt enjoyed brief periods of dominance, Persia eventually reconquered it in 343 BCE.

Language and communication also evolved during Persian rule. Aramaic replaced Hebrew as the spoken language in much of Palestine and became the region's lingua franca. The shift from Hebrew to Aramaic as the primary language of communication in Palestine during the Persian rule was not a sudden event but rather a gradual transition driven by various socio-political factors. The roots of this change can be traced back to the rise of the Aramean states during the late Bronze Age and their subsequent domination of large parts of the Near East.

Aramaic was the language of the Arameans, a Semitic people who originated in the region encompassing modern-day Syria and parts of Iraq, Lebanon, and Turkey. They established a number of independent kingdoms and city-states during the early first millennium BCE. In these areas, Aramaic was the primary language of public life, administration, and commerce.

In the 8th century BCE, the Assyrian Empire, which dominated the Near East, started employing Aramaic as a secondary language for administration, primarily due to its simplicity and flexibility compared to Akkadian. Thus, the widespread use of Aramaic was bolstered by Assyrian policy.

When the Neo-Babylonian Empire overtook the Assyrians, they maintained the use of Aramaic for similar reasons. When the Persians subsequently conquered Babylon, they continued to use Aramaic as the administrative language throughout their empire, which included Palestine. This widespread official usage of Aramaic across vast swaths of territory led to its adoption as a lingua franca, facilitating communication among the diverse ethnic and linguistic groups within the Persian Empire.

As a result, Aramaic gradually replaced Hebrew as the spoken language in much of Palestine. However, this did not mean the complete disappearance of Hebrew. In Judah, for instance, Hebrew persisted as the spoken language, although it was heavily influenced by Aramaic. The returning exiles from Babylon, who had been living in an environment where Aramaic was the dominant language, likely brought this influence back with them.

Nonetheless, Hebrew continued to hold a special place within the Israelite society. It remained the upper-class language and for religious purposes, such as in the writing of Torah scrolls and other religious texts. As such, the transition from Hebrew to Aramaic was less a complete linguistic replacement and more a bilingual situation, where both languages were used in different contexts and spheres of society.

Hellenistic Influence and Conflict

The late 330s BCE marked a key turning point in the history of Palestine, as Alexander the Great conquered the region on his way to Egypt. With the Persian control over Palestine weakening, the conquest was relatively straightforward, except for Tyre and Gaza. These two cities resisted Alexander's rule, which led to the slaughter of their citizens as punishment. The consequences of this conquest and the subsequent death of Alexander the Great in 323 BCE significantly reshaped the landscape of Palestine culturally, economically, and politically.

Following Alexander's death, his generals, the Diadochi, fought for control over his vast empire. During this turbulent period, two key figures emerged in the power struggle for Palestine: Ptolemy I Soter and Antigonus I Monophthalmus. Palestine changed hands multiple times over several decades, ultimately witnessing five wars between the Ptolemaic and the Seleucid Empires. By 201/200 BCE, the Seleucids conquered Palestine for good, establishing their territory in the region.

In stark contrast to previous Persian rule, the Seleucids brought Hellenistic culture to Palestine through a process called Hellenization. The introduction of Greek language, customs, religion, and architecture profoundly impacted the local population. Adopting Greek traditions and learning the language offered numerous advantages and opportunities for the upper classes. As such, Hellenization permeated various aspects of life, from the flourishing of Hellenistic pottery with Philistine elements to the growing influence of Greek values and culture in Palestine.

One of the most tangible expressions of Hellenistic influence in the region was the founding of Greek cities or Poleis. These cities granted their citizens exemptions from taxes and other privileges while exhibiting Greek-style governments, institutions, and places of worship. The Greeks often rebuilt and renamed existing cities, reflecting the Hellenistic era's rulers, such as Akko, which became Ptolemais (the region's capital during the Ptolemaic era), and Rabbath-Ammon, which was renamed Philadelphia after Ptolemy II Philadelphos. These Poleis' presence led to improved living standards for citizens and encouraged loyalty to the Hellenistic rulers.

It is essential to recognize that while there were undoubtedly benefits to Hellenistic rule, the influence of Greek culture was not universally accepted or embraced by the diverse population living within Palestine. Tensions arose between different ethnic and religious groups, while others remained steadfastly opposed to the incorporation of Hellenistic practices within their traditional ways of life. This persistent resistance eventually led to greater conflict within the region, notably the Maccabean Revolt.

In analyzing the impact of Hellenistic culture on Palestine, it is crucial to consider the complex and multifaceted nature of the changes that occurred during this period. The experiences of the local population – both those who embraced and those who resisted Hellenization – highlight the nuanced interaction between conquerors and the conquered, a dynamic that continues to shape the development of societies throughout history.

The Maccabean Revolt

The Maccabean Revolt began as a response to the aggressive campaign of repression against Jewish religious practices instituted by Seleucid King Antiochus IV Epiphanes in 168 BCE. It appears that Antiochus mistakenly believed an internal conflict among Jewish priesthood to be a full-scale rebellion and sought to quell this perceived threat. He banned Jewish practices, placed Jerusalem under direct Seleucid control, and converted the Second Temple into a site for a syncretic Pagan-Jewish cult. This campaign of repression inadvertently led to the very revolt he had feared.

The revolt was spearheaded by Judas Maccabeus, whose name "Maccabeus" translates to "The Hammer," in 167 BCE. Over time, their group of rebels would come to be known as the Maccabees, and their actions would later be documented in the books of 1 Maccabees and 2 Maccabees. Initially, the rebellion consisted of guerrilla movements raiding towns in the Judean countryside and terrorizing Greek officials beyond Seleucid control. Eventually, the rebel forces grew into a proper army capable of engaging the fortified cities occupied by the Seleucid Empire.

In 164 BCE, a significant early victory occurred when the Maccabees recaptured Jerusalem. This momentous event led to the cleansing of the temple and the rededication of the altar on 25 Kislev, which is commemorated in the festival of Hanukkah. Though the Seleucids eventually gave in and rescinded their ban on Judaism, the more radical factions within the Maccabee ranks were not satisfied with restoring Jewish practices under Seleucid rule. They demanded a complete break from the Seleucids and continued to fight for their independence.

Judas Maccabeus had scored several significant victories against the Seleucid forces and had even managed to cleanse and rededicate the Temple in Jerusalem, an event commemorated by the Jewish holiday of Hanukkah. His leadership was instrumental in maintaining the Jewish rebellion and preserving their religious and cultural autonomy.

However, the Battle of Elasa signaled a turning point in the Maccabean Revolt. Judas Maccabeus faced the Seleucid general Bacchides, who had been sent by King Demetrius I of the Seleucid Empire to quell the revolt. According to the account in the First Book of Maccabees, despite being heavily outnumbered, Judas chose to engage in battle to achieve another miraculous victory. Unfortunately, the Jewish forces were defeated, and Judas Maccabeus was killed.

This victory allowed Seleucid forces to regain direct control over the region, if only temporarily. Despite losing their charismatic leader, the Maccabean forces did not surrender. Judas' brother, Jonathan Apphus, assumed leadership and continued their resistance from the countryside. Under Jonathan's guidance, the Maccabees transitioned to guerilla warfare tactics, engaging in smaller, more frequent skirmishes rather than large-scale battles, which allowed them to wear down the Seleucid forces slowly.

The opportunity for independence finally arrived in 141 BCE when Simon Thassi, another member of the Maccabees, successfully expelled the Greeks from Jerusalem's citadel. A strategic alliance with the Roman Republic further secured their new-found independence. Consequently, Simon established an independent Hasmonean kingdom, which would rule until the arrival of the Roman Empire.

The Maccabean Revolt had far-reaching and long-lasting impacts on Jewish history. It served as a powerful example of a successful campaign to establish political independence and resist governmental suppression of Jewish religion and culture. Furthermore, the revolt greatly influenced Jewish nationalist sentiments and sowed the seeds for an ongoing struggle for religious freedom and political autonomy.

The Hasmonean Dynasty

The Hasmonean Dynasty, established in the tumultuous era of the 2nd century BCE, was an important chapter in the history of Palestine, as the region grappled with clashing empires and indigenous factions.

Capitalizing on the political divisions within the Seleucids, the Hasmoneans steadily began to augment their territory. They achieved semi-independence and gradually began extending their reign into neighboring regions. The territories of Perea, Samaria, Idumea, Galilee, and Iturea eventually came under their control.

John Hyrcanus, the third son of Simon and nephew of Judas Maccabeus, took on the dual role of High Priest and Ethnarch around 135 BCE. He also adopted a Greek name, demonstrating the Hasmoneans' acceptance of the culture. He was able to maintain a level of autonomy from the Seleucids, while also navigating complex political situations. The steady dissolution of the Seleucid Empire amid civil wars presented an opportunity for Hyrcanus. He exploited these circumstances to elevate the newly independent Hasmonean Kingdom, making significant military conquests including Madaba and Shechem.

As their territory expanded, so did the power and influence of the Hasmoneans. They ventured into roles that were not just limited to being rebel leaders, with Jonathan Apphus becoming the High Priest in 152 BCE, Simon Thassi taking the title of Ethnarch in 142 BCE, and eventually Aristobulus I being declared King in 104 BCE. This robust expansion brought unprecedented wealth and prestige to the Hasmonean kings and the temple institution in Jerusalem. However, their expansionist policies and forced conversions of conquered peoples created tensions that would later contribute to the downfall of Judea.

Upon the death of John Hyrcanus in 104 BCE, Aristobulus I took over. But his reign was short-lived, and he died of illness in 103 BCE. Despite the abrupt end to Aristobulus I's rule, the Hasmonean Dynasty continued to strengthen under Alexander Jannaeus. The expansion of the kingdom was relentless under his rule, with the conquest of Iturea and more territory along the Mediterranean coast.

Despite their successes, the Hasmoneans had to face significant losses and opposition from both within and outside their borders. Alexander Jannaeus faced a severe defeat at the Battle of Gadara in 93 BCE against the Nabataeans, leading to the loss of territories in Transjordan. The last ruler of the Hasmonean Dynasty was Salome Alexandra, who reigned from 76–67 BCE. She was the only reigning Jewish Queen of the Second Temple Era, and during her rule, her son Hyrcanus II served as the High Priest and was named as her successor.

The legacy of the Hasmonean Dynasty is indelible in the annals of Palestine's history. Despite the controversies and conflicts that marked their reign, the Hasmoneans remain a symbol of Jewish resilience against external powers. Their story provides important context for understanding the region's intricate religious, cultural, and political tapestry, which still resonates in the ongoing struggle for identity and independence in modern Palestine.

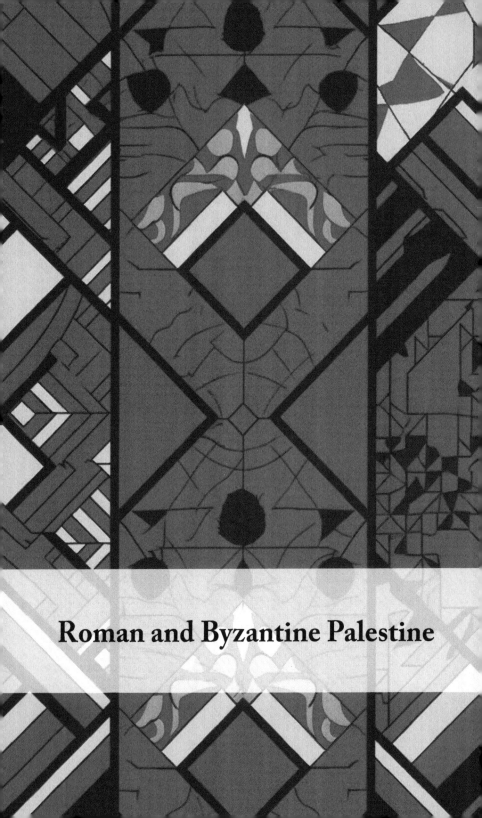

Roman and Byzantine Palestine

The echoes of the past still reverberate through the ancient land of Palestine, a place where empires once rose and fell, shaping the course of history and setting the stage for the unfolding narrative of the Middle East. As we stand at the edge of the modern era, peering back into the distant years of the Roman and Byzantine ages, we find a timeless tale of conquest and resistance, of destruction and rebirth. We are reminded that, in many ways, the struggles of the past remain intrinsically linked to the present, casting their long shadows over the hills and valleys where ancient cities once flourished.

It is within these storied lands that Rome extended its mighty grasp, seeking to bring order and stability under the banner of the empire. The Roman conquest and rule of Palestine would prove both challenging and transformative, demanding adaption not only of the conquerors but also of the conquered. How did these great imperial powers from afar manage the region's diverse cultures, religions, and identities, and how did they navigate the complexities of governance and diplomacy that came with such an undertaking? In the heart of the Jewish homeland, the seeds of rebellion were sown as factions, zealots, and revolutionaries rose up against their foreign overlords. The Jewish revolts serve as a testament to the unyielding spirit of a people unwilling to bend to the will of their conquerors, a spirit that culminated in a cataclysmic event that would forever change the course of Jewish history – the destruction of the Second Temple.

With the passing of centuries, the landscape of Palestine was reshaped once more under the influence of the Byzantine Empire. An era marked by the intricate dance between religious, political, and social dynamics as Christianity spread its roots across the Eastern Mediterranean. But how did Christianization and the Byzantine rule over Palestine mold the region and its people? How did it affect Judaism, which had long been the predominant faith of the land? The conversion of the region to Christianity triggered the immense construction of churches, monasteries, and the Holy Places, weaving the story of the faith into the very fabric of the land. During this time, dramatic developments were taking place just beyond the edges of the known world, and once again, Palestine would be witness to the arrival of new conquerors – the early Islamic forces.

As we delve into the intricate tapestry of Roman and Byzantine Palestine, our aim is to unravel the threads of history with objectivity and fairness, acknowledging the voices and perspectives of the diverse characters that have shaped this narrative. By exploring the motives, causes, and effects of the events that took place, we hope to deepen our understanding of this crucial period in human history, and by doing so, illuminate how it still resonates with our contemporary world. We invite you, the reader, to journey with us through this tale of empires, faith, and the enduring human spirit, as we turn the pages and discover the rich story that lies beneath the sands of time.

Roman Conquest and Rule

The Roman Conquest and Rule of Palestine was initiated amidst a power struggle in the Hasmonean court. In 63 BCE, two Hasmonean claimants were competing for the throne of the Jewish kingdom, which provided an opening for the Roman general Pompey to intervene. Pompey saw an opportunity to establish Roman influence in the region, an ambition that would result in centuries of Roman rule in Palestine.

Pompey, one of the most influential figures of his time, had been slowly extending Roman influence in the Eastern Mediterranean. He had been involved in a successful campaign against the pirates plaguing the Mediterranean, and in a series of wars against Mithridates VI of Pontus, a persistent enemy of Rome. After subduing the Kingdom of Pontus and incorporating it into the Roman province of Asia, Pompey turned his attention towards Syria and Judea.

Arriving in the land in 63 BCE, Pompey was presented with an opportunity to extend Roman control further. He had been welcomed by the representatives of both Hasmonean factions, who hoped to secure his support in their familial dispute. Rather than picking a side, Pompey exploited the internal conflict for Rome's advantage. He decided to intervene under the pretext of restoring peace, launching a military campaign against Jerusalem.

The Battle of Jerusalem was a challenging siege for Pompey and his forces. The city was heavily fortified, and the defenders, primarily supporters of Aristobulus II, were determined to resist. The Roman legions, however, were renowned for their siegecraft. After a three-month-long blockade, they finally breached the city's defenses, entering the city and the sacred Second Temple.

The aftermath was brutal. Pompey installed Hyrcanus II, the more pliant of the Hasmonean brothers, as High Priest, effectively making him a Roman client. However, he deliberately withheld the title of king from Hyrcanus II, a decision that asserted Rome's political dominance.

With the Roman conquest, the landscape of the region changed significantly. The territories under Judea now only consisted of Judea proper, Samaria (minus the city of Samaria, now renamed Sebaste), southern Galilee, and eastern Idumaea. In the wake of the unrest, the Romans took further steps to assert control in 57 BCE. They collaborated with Jewish loyalists to stamp out an uprising organized by Hyrcanus II's rivals and systematically restructured the kingdom into five autonomous districts, complete with their own religious councils. Centers for these districts were established in Jerusalem, Sepphoris, Jericho, Amathus, and Gadara.

These reforms secured Roman control and led to the revival of many Greek cities previously occupied or destroyed by the Hasmoneans. These cities, now granted self-governing status, became Rome's loyal regional ally. In appreciation, they adopted new dating systems that commemorated Rome's advent, named themselves after Roman officials, and minted coins bearing the names and images of Roman officials.

However, the Roman civil wars that erupted around this time would impact Rome's hold on Judea. In 40 BCE, the

Parthian Empire, along with their Jewish ally Antigonus the Hasmonean, took advantage of the unstable environment and defeated the pro-Roman Jewish forces led by high priest Hyrcanus II, Phasael, and Herod I, son of Hyrcanus' leading supporter Antipater. With the support of the Parthians, Antigonus' forces successfully conquered Syria and Palestine, and Antigonus was crowned King of Judea.

Herod I, recognizing the need for further Roman support, fled to Rome and was elected "King of the Jews" by the Roman Senate. He was tasked with retaking Judea and, in 37 BCE, managed to wrest back control of the region with the help of Roman forces. This marked the end of the short-lived Hasmonean resurgence and set a new era of Roman control in motion.

The Roman Conquest and Rule significantly shifted the region's politics, culture, and administration. Jerusalem, which had once served as a powerful Hasmonean stronghold, had its identity and influence transformed under Roman rule. The consequences of this intervention would reverberate throughout the history of Palestine, setting the stage for the Jewish revolts, the destruction of the Second Temple, and the region's eventual integration into the Byzantine and early Islamic empires.

Jewish Revolts

The Jewish-Roman Wars were characterized by a series of revolts that took place between 66 and 135 CE. The First Jewish–Roman War, fought from 66 to 73 CE, and the Bar Kokhba Revolt, waged between 132 and 136 CE, were largely driven by nationalist aspirations. Jews in these conflicts aimed to restore an independent Judean state, free from Roman rule.

The First Jewish-Roman War saw the emergence of several key figures and events. Principally, it involved the resistance of Jewish factions against the mighty Roman Empire, led by the likes of General Vespasian and his son, Titus. Despite initial successes in driving the Romans out of Jerusalem, mounting internal conflicts among the Jewish factions ultimately weakened their efforts.

After four years of conflict, Roman legions led by Titus retook and destroyed much of Jerusalem, including the Second Temple, on 4 August 70 CE or 30 August 70 CE. This date is possibly the same day on which Tisha B'Av, an annual fast day in Judaism, was observed.

The Arch of Titus, built in Rome to commemorate Titus's victory over the Jews in Judea, depicts a Roman victory procession where soldiers carry spoils from the destroyed Temple, including the Menorah. It is also inscribed on the Colosseum that Emperor Vespasian built it using war spoils in 79 CE, which may have come from the destruction of the Second Temple.

The aftermath of the Second Temple's destruction greatly affected the religious landscape of the time. The sects of Judaism that had their base in the Temple significantly dwindled in importance, including the priesthood and the Sadducees. Much of today's religious practices can be traced back to the Pharisee movement, which continued after the urban devastation.

The Temple's former location is now the Dome of the Rock site, with its gates leading out close to Al-Aqsa Mosque, which was built many years later. Despite the destruction, Jews continued to live in Jerusalem, but their presence declined following Emperor Hadrian's establishment of a new city called Aelia Capitolina. In the aftermath of the Bar Kokhba revolt in 135 CE, many Jewish communities were massacred, and Jews were forbidden from residing within Jerusalem's borders. A pagan Roman temple was even constructed on the site of Herod's Temple.

Historical accounts, such as the works of Josephus, detail that not only was the Jewish Temple destroyed, but the entirety of Jerusalem's Lower City as well. Still, some structures were spared, such as the Tower of Phasael, now inaccurately called the Tower of David. These structures were preserved as a memorial to the city's strength. The Midrash Rabba recounts an episode where Rabban Yohanan ben Zakkai asked Vespasian to spare the westernmost gates of the city during the Roman siege. These gates, leading to Lydda, were similarly saved from destruction by the Arab auxiliaries who fought alongside the Romans.

Different from the First war, the Kitos War (115-117 CE) was based more on ethno-religious tensions. Although also a part of the larger narrative of the Jewish-Roman Wars, this conflict occurred primarily outside of the Judea province, hence some sources distinguishing it from other Jewish-Roman conflicts. Throughout this period, Jews faced immense persecution in various Mediterranean cities leading to much anger and causing them to fight for relief against Roman authorities.

The Bar Kokhba Revolt, which took place between 132 and 136 CE, was a monumental event in the history of the Jewish people. This rebellion, also known as the Third Jewish-Roman War or the "Jewish Expedition" in Roman accounts, represented the final and arguably most severe of the major Jewish uprisings against Roman rule.

Simon Bar Kokhba, the leader of the revolt, was a charismatic figure who managed to unite various Jewish factions under a common cause. He was perceived by many as the Messiah, the one destined to liberate the Jewish people and restore their national independence. In a swift and robust display of power, the rebellion under Bar Kokhba's leadership spread quickly across Judea, resulting in several early victories against Roman forces. These successes enabled the rebels to establish an independent state over much of the region, known as the "House of Israel", where Bar Kokhba assumed the title of Nasi, or "head of state."

However, these early victories did not go unanswered. The Roman Emperor Hadrian mobilized a massive counter-offensive force, comprised of six full legions, along with auxiliaries and elements from up to six additional legions. Under the command of General Julius Severus, this substantial Roman force gradually crushed the rebellion, culminating in the capture of the rebel stronghold in 136 CE.

The consequences of the Bar Kokhba Revolt were profound and far-reaching. For the Jewish population of Judea, the impact was devastating. While exact numbers are hard to ascertain, Cassius Dio, a Roman historian, reported that 580,000 Jews were killed in the battles, with many more succumbing to hunger and disease. In addition to this, many Jews were expelled from Judea, and a significant number of captives were sold into slavery. The sheer scale of the losses led to substantial demographic changes, with the Jewish demographic and cultural center shifting from Judea to Galilee. Some scholars argue that this was the moment when Jews became a minority in the Land of Israel.

Roman forces, too, suffered heavy losses. So much so that the Roman legion known as XXII Deiotariana was disbanded, likely due to severe casualties. Despite these losses, Hadrian's counter-offensive had effectively quelled the rebellion, solidifying Rome's control over Judea.

The aftermath of the revolt also marked significant shifts in Jewish religious thought. The brutal defeat led to a recalibration of Jewish messianism, shifting it from a tangible, political concept to a more abstract and spiritual one. Bar Kokhba, once hailed as the Messiah, was referred to in the Talmud as "Ben-Kusiba," a derogatory term meaning "son of deception," highlighting his status as a false Messiah.

Furthermore, the revolt played a pivotal role in the divergence of Christianity as a separate religion from Judaism. Given the severe oppression faced by the Jews following the revolt, the Christian community increasingly sought to distinguish itself from its Jewish roots. As a consequence of the revolt, the Romans barred Jews from Jerusalem, except for attendance during Tisha B'Av, thereby creating a physical and symbolic separation between the two faiths.

These Jewish-Roman Wars had dramatic consequences for the Jewish people and their religion. With the Second Temple in ruins, Jews faced the challenge of finding new ways to practice their faith, eventually leading to Rabbinic Judaism. Furthermore, Jews became a scattered and persecuted minority across the Eastern Mediterranean, leading to a diaspora that dispersed Jews across various regions.

In analyzing the Jewish-Roman Wars, particularly the First Jewish-Roman War and the Bar Kokhba Revolt, it is crucial to emphasize the nationalist aspect of these conflicts. The struggle for an independent Jewish state against the Roman Empire was the driving force behind the rebellions. At the same time, it is important to consider the ethno-religious component that defined the Kitos War and the persecution and oppression of the Jewish people that contributed to their revolutionary efforts.

Ultimately, the Jewish-Roman Wars significantly impacted the Jewish people, transforming their society, religious practices, and presence in the Eastern Mediterranean. Understanding these revolts is crucial in framing the narrative of the Palestinian history, which would later see the Jewish people reclaim their homeland after millennia in exile.

Byzantine Rule and Christianization

The 4th century witnessed a significant shift in Christianity's favor, with the religion transforming from being heavily persecuted to becoming the Roman state church. Constantine the Great played an instrumental role in this change by defeating his competitors in a series of civil wars, attributing his victories to Christianity. As Rome's first Christian emperor, he supported the church and its clergy by granting them fiscal and legal privileges and immunities, endorsing ecumenical councils to settle disputes within the faith.

This profound impact on Christianity extended to Palestine, as churches were constructed on sites of importance. Examples include the Church of the Holy Sepulchre in Jerusalem and the Church of the Nativity in Bethlehem. During this period, over 140 Christian monasteries were established in Palestine, with Mar Saba, Saint George's Monastery in Wadi Qelt, and the Monastery of the Temptation near Jericho among the world's oldest. As men flocked to live as hermits in the Judean wilderness, Palestine became a center for eremitic life. The ecumenical council in Chalcedon in 451 elevated Jerusalem to a patriarchate and one of the five self-governing centers for Christianity, significantly enhancing the international stature of the Palestinian church.

The Byzantine era in Palestine brought prosperity and cultural flourishing. Urbanization increased, with new areas cultivated and numerous cities experiencing peak populations. Towns developed new civic basilicas and porticoed streets with space for shops, stimulating the economy due to a boom in the construction of religious structures. The total population of Palestine may have exceeded 1.5 million during this period, a peak that would not be reached again until the 20th century.

Caesarea and Gaza emerged as essential learning centers, rivaling the academies of Alexandria and Athens. Christian scholars made significant contributions to rhetoric, historiography, church history, and hagiography. Saint Jerome's translation of the Old Testament into Latin, known as the Vulgate, became the Catholic Church's officially promulgated version. Eusebius' Onomasticon helped conceptualize the Western view of Palestine as the Christian Holy Land.

Administrative and political changes occurred as well, with smaller provincial units and regional groups called dioceses emerging to facilitate efficient governance. Palestine was reorganized into the provinces Palaestina Prima, Palaestina Secunda, and Palaestina Tertia or Palaestina Salutaris.

Jewish communities thrived in the region, though their share of the population likely decreased during Byzantine rule. Notably, Emperor Julian attempted to reverse Christianity's influence in 361, ordering the Jewish temple in Jerusalem to be rebuilt. However, the re-establishment of Christian dominance following his death in 363 ended these efforts.

Christian Arab tribes, such as the Ghassanids, became the largest Arab group in Palestine during this period. They migrated from South Arabia and created two client kingdoms in Palaestina Secunda and Palaestina Tertia, serving as Byzantine buffer zones.

The Samaritans and Jews revolted against Christian dominance several times in the late 5th and early 6th centuries, driven by discrimination against non-Christians. These revolts were quelled, solidifying Christian control over Palestine.

In the early 7th century, warfare between the Byzantine and Persian Empires escalated. The Persians invaded the Levant, inciting Jewish revolts against the Byzantines. Persian-Jewish forces captured Jerusalem in 614, but by 617, the Persians sided with the Christian majority and reclaimed the city. Roman Emperor Heraclius triumphantly returned the True Cross to Jerusalem in 629. However, enduring conflict took its toll on both empires, paving the way for the Arab conquests a decade later.

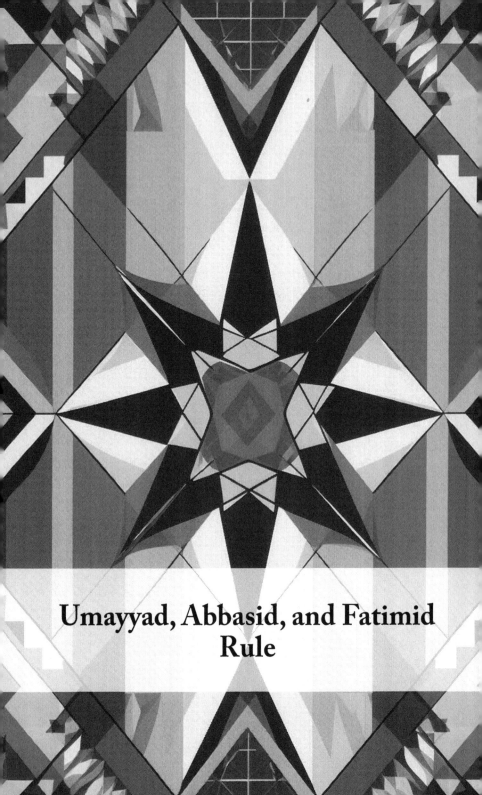

Umayyad, Abbasid, and Fatimid Rule

An influential and transformative period in world history unfolded. It was a time when powerful dynasties rose and fell, lasting religious institutions took root, and ground-breaking innovations in science, architecture, and the arts flourished. This captivating era, known as the Early Islamic Era, spans between the 7th and 12th centuries CE. Our journey will focus on three influential caliphates that governed vast territories: the Umayyad, the Abbasid, and the Fatimid.

The story begins with the Umayyad Caliphate, a trailblazing Islamic state that emerged from Mecca and Medina's sands. An architectural marvel, the Dome of the Rock, punctuates this era with its stunning design. A symbol of the Umayyad's political prowess, this illustrious structure represents the first monumental work of Islamic art and architecture. Subsequently, a period of political upheaval and rebellion follows, ultimately paving the way for Abbasid rule.

The Abbasid Caliphate marked a new chapter in the Islamic world. As a golden age in many spheres of life, it was marked by a breathtaking cultural renaissance, scientific achievements, and a burgeoning exchange of ideas. From trade and translation to intricate geometric patterns, the Abbasid era revolutionized the world from Baghdad's bustling city streets.

However, the Islamic world was not without its dissenters. To the west, the Fatimid Caliphate blossomed as a distinctive offshoot of the Islamic tradition. Their form of governance was a fascinating mixture of religion and politics, as their caliphs both claimed descendant from the Prophet

Muhammad and the rightful claim to leading the Muslim world. This era bore witness to intense sectarian struggles, with the Fatimid dynasty's religious positioning sharply contrasting with that of their Sunni counterparts.

Amidst the fascinating tug of war between the devout and the pragmatic, trudged the footsteps of outsiders. The story cannot be told without casting light upon the fateful impact of the Crusader Incursions. European Christians seeking to reclaim the Holy Land unleashed a wave of violence that would ultimately shape the dynamics of this intricate historical period.

It would not be long before a new force emerged to confront the external threat. Among the vast sands and arid landscapes, the determined Ayyubids would rise to reassert their vision of an Islamic order. As they fought to reclaim land from the Crusaders, the landscape of the region transformed, marking yet another pivotal shift in the ever-evolving story of the Early Islamic Era.

As we explore these exciting tales—shrouded in conquests, innovations, and resilient faith—we are faced with an unspoken challenge: to recognize the past's relevance to the present. In particular, the influence of these caliphates persists today, as the political, religious, and cultural landscapes they shaped continue to reverberate across much of the world. By understanding these complex dynamics, we may begin to appreciate the inextricable link between peoples of the past, their beliefs, struggles, and triumphs, and the echoes of their actions in today's world.

Early Islamic Conquests

The Early Islamic Conquests marked a transformative period in the history of Palestine, a land that had long been dominated by Roman and Byzantine rule. The rapid expansion of Islam in the 7th century led to the unprecedented rise of a new power in the region, culminating in the establishment of Islamic rule over much of Palestine. This chapter delves into the political, military, and cultural dimensions of the Early Islamic Conquests, exploring the factors that spurred its successes and the lasting impact of these momentous events on the region and its peoples.

The historical backdrop of the Islamic expansion plays a crucial role in understanding the events that unfolded in Palestine. The rise of Islam in the Arabian Peninsula under the leadership of the Prophet Muhammad unified the Arab tribes and brought forth a newfound sense of purpose and unity. Under the leadership of the early Caliphs, particularly Abu Bakr and Umar ibn al-Khattab, the Islamic state expanded rapidly, with its armies defeating the Sassanid Persian Empire and challenging the Byzantine Empire for the control of the Levant, including Palestine.

During this time, numerous campaigns and battles defined the Islamic conquest of Palestine. Key leaders, such as Khalid ibn al-Walid and Amr ibn al-As, played crucial roles in achieving military success. Islamic forces utilized diplomacy to secure alliances with various local tribes, while technological advancements, including advances in siege warfare, helped the Islamic armies capture major cities like Jerusalem and Caesarea. The Battle of Yarmouk, near the border of modern-day Syria and Jordan, proved decisive in solidifying Islamic dominance in the region.

The reaction of local populations to the Islamic conquests was complex and varied. Jewish communities, who had suffered persecution under Byzantine rule, often welcomed the Islamic conquerors as liberators, offering support and assistance. Some Christian communities in Palestine also sought to cooperate with the new Islamic rulers, hoping to alleviate the heavy taxes and restrictions imposed by the Byzantine Empire. However, conflicts and tensions were also present, with instances of resistance and opposition to the Islamic expansion.

In the aftermath of the conquests, Islamic rule in Palestine brought about significant changes in the administrative, religious, and cultural spheres. The new rulers established Arabic as the official language and implemented Islamic law, while maintaining religious tolerance towards the Jewish and Christian communities. Many non-Muslims converted to Islam, often driven by social and economic incentives, which prompted the growth of Islamic religious institutions such as mosques and madrasas.

Maintaining stability and consolidating control over Palestine posed challenges to the early Islamic rulers. Internal disputes, particularly the escalating conflict between the Umayyad and Abbasid factions, undermined the unity of the Islamic state. Simultaneously, external threats from the Byzantine Empire persisted, with several attempts to retake Palestine, such as the siege of Tyre in the 7th century.

Historiographical debates on the Islamic conquests of Palestine revolve around the extent and nature of the changes brought forth by the new rulers. Some historians have stressed the transformative aspects of the conquest, highlighting the disruptions and changes to the social, economic, and political structures of the region. Others have emphasized the continuities that persisted through the period, as the conquerors often adopted elements from the previous administrations to consolidate their rule.

The Early Islamic Conquests established an enduring Islamic presence in Palestine that has resonated throughout the centuries. The subsequent ruling dynasties, such as the Umayyads, Abbasids, and Fatimids, continued to shape the religious, political, and cultural landscape of the land, leaving behind a rich tapestry of Islamic heritage. The contemporary issues faced by modern-day Palestinians, pertaining to territorial disputes and identity politics, cannot be fully understood without acknowledging the profound impact of the Early Islamic Conquests in shaping the historical narrative of Palestine.

Umayyad Caliphate and Dome of the Rock

The rise of Islam in the late 6th century brought significant change and development to the landscape of Palestine. Prophet Muhammad's founding of the Islamic faith and the unification of Arabian tribes led to the formation of the caliphate. This religious polity would continue to expand into an empire through jihad, or holy war. The conquest of Palestine occurred between 636 and 640, ushering in a new era under Islamic rule.

Society within the caliphate was structured into a pyramid of five tiers, with Arabs at the top, converts to Islam below them, and non-Muslim members of society, such as dhimmis, free men, and slaves forming the remaining layers. Dhimmis, "protected persons" like Christians, Jews, and Samaritans, were allowed to practice their religion in peace, although they were subject to certain restrictions and a special tax called jizya.

Under Islamic rule, the territory of the Byzantine Dioceses Orientes was organized into five military districts, or junds. Palestine was divided into Jund Filastin and Jund al-Urdunn, with the city of Ramla serving as the administrative capital of Jund Filastin. Throughout the period of Umayyad rule, Palestine became a prosperous region due to its strategic location for international trade, influx of pilgrims, agricultural productivity, and local craftsmanship.

Despite being under Muslim control, the Christian world maintained a strong attachment to the Holy Land, demonstrated by donations to holy sites and the facilitation of

Christian pilgrimage. However, dangers such as attacks by highwaymen would later inspire the Crusaders to "liberate" Jerusalem in the name of protecting Christian pilgrims.

In 656, the assassination of Rashidun caliph Uthman ignited the first civil war within the caliphate. The Umayyad dynasty emerged victorious, moving the capital from Kufa to Damascus. This shift placed a greater focus on the nearby city of Jerusalem and its significance to the Islamic faith. Two important religious structures were built on the Temple Mount: the al-Jami'a al-Aqsa and the Dome of the Rock, both of which remain significant to this day.

The long-standing feud between Arab tribal confederations, the Qays and the Yaman, began under Umayyad rule and persisted throughout Palestine's history. Conflicts and uprisings between these groups continued well into the 19th century, with the caliphate struggling to keep tensions under control.

The era of Umayyad rule significantly shaped Palestine's development, introducing new religious and cultural influences to the region while retaining connections to its Christian past. As the oldest extant Islamic monument, the Dome of the Rock remains a symbol of the importance of Jerusalem and the dynamic history of this unique part of the world.

Abbasid Rule and Cultural Influence

The rise of the Abbasids marked a significant shift in power dynamics within the Islamic world. After overthrowing the Umayyad Caliphate in 750, the Abbasids held their power base in Persia and moved the capital from Damascus to Baghdad in 762. The change of the capital meant that Palestine lost its central position within the caliphate and became a province on the periphery whose problems were not tended to with great care. Although this did not result in an immediate decline in the region, it ended the Umayyads' extravagant investments in Palestine.

Under Abbasid rule, the once influential tribes of Syria, including those from Palestine who had supported the Umayyads, lost their sway in the caliphate's political affairs. While these tribes no longer held significant influence, they continued to participate in various rebellions that plagued the Abbasid rule. Rebellions and other disturbances constantly troubled the Abbasids' governance in Palestine. In the 790s, the Qays-Yaman feud led to several wars in the region. Violence between Qaysi rebels and the Yamani and Abbasid regime continued to escalate, with significant force needed to quell the battles. Another uprising, led by the Yaman Al-Mubarqa, erupted in the 840s, rousing peasants and tribesmen against the Abbasid regime. These outbreaks of violence were highly destructive, causing substantial havoc as rebels looted monasteries and devastated cities. Consequently, Palestine was often lawless during this period.

By the end of the 9th century, the Abbasids began to lose control of their western provinces due to internal instability. In 873, Ahmad Ibn Tulun, the governor of Egypt, declared independence and founded the Tulunid dynasty. Later, he occupied Syria. Under Tulunid rule, the persecution of Christians ceased, prompteding the renovation of churches in Jerusalem and the port of Acre. Despite these positive developments, the Tulunids' rule was brief; by 906, the Abbasids had regained control of Palestine.

The Abbasids' control lasted until 939 when they granted autonomous control of Egypt and Palestine to Muhammad ibn Tughj al-Ikhshid, who then established the Ikshidid dynasty. The Ikshidids' rule was marred by instances of persecution against Christians, sometimes with the support of local Jews. In 937, the Church of the Resurrection was plundered and set ablaze, while in 966, severe anti-Christian riots occurred in Jerusalem. This period of unrest persisted, with anarchy reigning after the death of the Ikhshidid regent in 968. Ultimately, many welcomed the Fatimid Caliphate's conquest of the Ikhshid state in 969.

Through this tumultuous period of Abbasid rule in Palestine, it becomes evident that the region experienced significant transformations in its political landscape, society, and religious dynamics. The loss of central influence, internal strife, and power struggles eventually paved the way for the rise and fall of various local powers, which proved instrumental in shaping the future of Palestine.

Fatimid Rule and Sectarian Struggles

The Fatimid Caliphate, which was established in North Africa in the early 10th century, expanded its territory by conquering the Ikshidids in 969. This marked the beginning of Fatimid control over Palestine, albeit a precarious one. The following decades were characterized by near-constant warfare between the Fatimid Caliphate and various competing factions, including the Byzantine Empire, the Qarmatians, Bedouin tribes such as the Jarrahids, and internal strife between Berber and Turkic factions within the Fatimid army. These conflicts took a heavy toll on the people and the land, causing widespread death and destruction.

During this time, the Bedouin tribes managed to gain considerable power and autonomy in Palestine, particularly between 997 and 1010. This period was marked by several uprisings and power struggles, with the Jarrahid tribe successfully asserting de facto independent rule over much of the region during key intervals in 977-982, 1011-1013, and 1024-1029. The rule of the Bedouin tribes brought about extensive pillaging and atrocities which severely impacted Palestine.

In the early 11th century, the Fatimid Caliph Al-Hakim bi-Amr Allah initiated a campaign of religious persecution, ordering the demolition of churches and synagogues across his empire, which included the Church of the Holy Sepulchre. Christian Europe responded with shock and outrage, casting blame upon the Jewish people. Al-Hakim also mandated that Christians and Jews wear distinctive clothing, signaling an intensification of existing policies regarding the treatment of non-Muslim populations. These policies were likely fueled by a combination of factors, such as critiques of Al-Hakim's father's more liberal stance towards the protected non-Muslim populations, or "dhimmi," as well as political pressure from the Byzantine Empire. Despite his persecution, access to the Holy Sepulchre was eventually restored, though repression of non-Muslim communities persisted.

In the mid-11th century, the Seljuk Turks invaded West Asia, leading to territorial losses for both the Byzantine Empire and the Fatimid Caliphate. Palestine found itself once again embroiled in anarchy and warfare as various factions vied for control. The Seljuk rule in Palestine, initiated by their conquest in 1071-1073, was a time marked by significant bloodshed, devastation, and economic difficulty. A popular uprising against the Seljuks in 1077 was brutally suppressed, resulting in massacres in Jerusalem, Gaza, Ramla, and Jaffa. The Fatimids eventually succeeded in retaking Jerusalem from the Seljuks in 1098, briefly reintroducing some semblance of stability to the region.

Further complicating the already tumultuous 11th century, Palestine experienced three major earthquakes in 1015, 1033, and 1068. The latter proved particularly disastrous for the region, killing around 15,000 people and virtually leveling the city of Ramla.

This period of Fatimid rule, marked by chaos, violence, and destruction, offers insight into contemporary issues within modern-day Palestine. Power struggles, conflicts, and sectarian tensions have deep historical roots that continue to shape the present-day social, political, and cultural landscape of the region. Understanding this tumultuous historical context can enhance our understanding of the longstanding challenges faced by the people of Palestine and the broader Middle East.

Crusader Incursions

The Crusades, a sequence of military campaigns endorsed by the Papacy of the Christian Europe, were aimed at regaining control of the Holy Land, particularly Palestine, from Muslim rule. These crusades were stimulated by several factors, including restrictions on pilgrimage routes, the evolution of doctrines that sanctified war in the name of religion, and a push to bridge the divide between the Eastern and Western branches of Christianity. It was in this backdrop that the First Crusade emerged, the most successful of all the Crusades, setting a precedent that would be followed by numerous other such campaigns.

The First Crusade, which lasted from 1096 to 1099, stands as the inaugural instance of these religious wars, which were initiated, supported, and at times directed by the Latin Church in the medieval era. The central aim was to liberate the Holy Land from Islamic governance. Despite Jerusalem being under Muslim rule for centuries, by the 11th century, the Seljuk Turks' takeover of the region posed a threat to local Christian populations, the pilgrimage routes from the West, and the Byzantine Empire.

The initial call for the First Crusade took place in 1095, when Byzantine emperor Alexios I Komnenos appealed for military aid from the Council of Piacenza against the Seljuk Turks. Later that year, Pope Urban II at the Council of Clermont seconded the Byzantine request for help, but also encouraged Christians to embark on an armed pilgrimage to Jerusalem. This call was met with widespread enthusiasm across all classes of Western Europe.

A surge of mainly lower-class Christians, led by French priest Peter the Hermit, was the first to respond, thus triggering the People's Crusade. However, this movement also witnessed some brutal anti-Jewish incidents, such as the Rhineland massacres, and ultimately suffered a disastrous defeat at the Battle of Civetot in October 1096.

Following the People's Crusade, the Princes' Crusade was initiated, which saw a significant number of nobility and their followers begin their journey towards Constantinople between November 1096 and April 1097. This Crusade comprised notable Western European princes, their followers, and as many as 100,000 non-combatants. Through a series of battles and sieges, they gradually reached Jerusalem and took control of the city in July 1099.

In 1187, the reign of the Holy Land was seized by the Ayyubid dynasty, who managed to capture Palestine, including the profoundly significant city of Jerusalem. This historical turning point was orchestrated under the leadership of the renowned Muslim general, Saladin. However, despite their significant victory, the Ayyubids could not conquer the resilient city of Tyre and the northern Crusader states. This led to a subsequent Crusade, which by 1192 had reclaimed most of the Palestinian coast.

The Siege of Jerusalem, which took place from 20 September to 2 October 1187, was a pivotal event in this period. Saladin, after having defeated the kingdom's army and captured numerous cities earlier that summer, laid siege to the city. Balian of Ibelin, entrusted with organizing a defense, found the city teeming with refugees but sorely lacking in soldiers. Yet, the defenders managed to rebuff several assaults by Saladin's army. The city was eventually surrendered to Saladin, but not before Balian negotiated safe passage for many of its inhabitants, resulting in limited bloodshed.

Saladin's rule in Jerusalem was marked by a certain degree of tolerance towards Christians, showcasing a conciliatory approach not often seen in times of conflict. He not only restored Muslim holy sites in Jerusalem, but also allowed Orthodox and Eastern Christian pilgrims to freely visit the sacred sites—however, Frankish or Catholic pilgrims were obliged to pay an entry fee. The management of Christian affairs in the city was handed over to the Ecumenical Patriarch of Constantinople.

Although Jerusalem remained under Ayyubid control, the Third Crusade, launched in 1189, shifted the power dynamic. Spearheaded by eminent leaders such as Richard the Lionheart, Philip Augustus, and Frederick Barbarossa, the Crusaders reconquered the Palestinian coast, although Jerusalem was not recaptured until the Sixth Crusade.

However, the Crusaders' success was fleeting. A crushing defeat at the Battle of La Forbie in 1244 severely diminished Latin influence in the region. By 1291, the Mamluks had decimated Acre, the capital of the Kingdom of Jerusalem. Despite the city's fall, the Treaty of Jaffa ensured that pilgrims retained access to the Church of the Holy Sepulchre. The complex history of Jerusalem, marked by conquests, defeats, and treaties, mirrors the turbulent and rich history of the region itself.

European interest in crusading gradually diminished over time due to shifting ideas about Christian life and the emergence of heretical beliefs within Europe. Meanwhile, the establishment of military orders such as the Knights Templar and the Hospitallers contributed to the defense and continued Crusader presence in the region, providing stability in Palestine despite multiple campaigns.

Crusader rule left a significant architectural impact on Palestine. Numerous fortifications, castles, towers, and fortified villages were constructed in both rural and urban areas, with remnants of this era still visible in places like Acre's old city. Additionally, the Jewish population in Palestine played a vital role in resisting the Crusaders and faced varying levels of hardship during this period. Some Jews fought alongside Muslims against the Crusaders in battles such as Jerusalem in 1099 and Haifa in 1100.

The Crusader incursions in the history of Palestine offer a compelling narrative that highlights various motives, causes, and consequences of this complex period of warfare between European Christians and the region's Muslim inhabitants. Today, these historical accounts continue to provide perspective and contextualize the complexities of religious and cultural struggles that have shaped and influenced the region over time.

Ayyubid Conquest and Reassertion of Islam

Under Ayyubid rule, Palestine experienced a period of religious tolerance and unity. The Ayyubids allowed Jewish and Orthodox Christian settlement in the region while also converting the Dome of the Rock back into an Islamic center of worship. The Mosque of Omar was constructed under Saladin outside the Church of the Holy Sepulchre, commemorating Umar the Great's decision to pray outside the church to safeguard its status as a Christian site.

The Ayyubid reign in Palestine eventually gave way to the Mamluk Sultanate, originating in Egypt as a consequence of the Seventh Crusade. This Crusade, initiated in response to the destruction of Jerusalem in 1244, ultimately failed with the defeat and capture of Louis IX of France by Ayyubid Sultan Turanshah at the Battle of Fariskur in 1250. A month later, Mamluk soldiers killed Turanshah, and his stepmother, Shajar al-Durr, became Sultana of Egypt with the Mamluk Aybak as Atabeg. The Ayyubids then relocated to Damascus, where they continued to govern Palestine for an additional ten years.

During the late 13th century, Palestine and Syria became the central front against the rapidly expanding Mongol Empire. Mongol forces first reached Palestine in 1260 and commenced their raids under the leadership of the Nestorian Christian general Kitbuqa. Hulagu Khan later informed Louis IX of France that Jerusalem was under the Franco-Mongol Alliance. However, Hulagu Khan had to return to Mongolia following the death of Mongke, leaving

Kitbuqa with a weakened army. Consequently, the Mamluks defeated the remaining Mongol forces under Baibars at the Battle of Ain Jalut in the Jezreel Valley. This crucial victory marked the zenith of Mongol conquests, although they managed to execute several more minor raids up to 1300, reaching as far as Gaza.

Both the Ayyubids and the Mamluks employed a strategic policy of destroying coastal areas in Palestine, rendering many cities, from Tyre in the north to Gaza in the south, desolate and non-operational. This calculated move sought to deter potential attacks from the sea and prevent the resurgence of Crusader forces. Consequently, these regions remained sparsely populated for centuries, with activity shifting more inland.

Under Mamluk rule, Palestine was part of the Damascus Wilayah and divided into three smaller sanjaks with capitals in Jerusalem, Gaza, and Safed. Palestine's population dwindled to around 200,000 due to ongoing conflicts, natural disasters, and the Black Death. Despite these challenges, the Mamluks established a "postal road" connecting Cairo and Damascus, which provided lodging for travelers and essential infrastructure, such as bridges. In addition, many schools were constructed, and previously neglected or destroyed mosques were renovated.

In 1377, a revolt erupted in the major cities of Palestine and Syria, which was eventually suppressed. This contributed to Barquq's coup d'etat in Cairo in 1382, resulting in the establishment of the Mamluk Burji dynasty. This period saw Palestine celebrated by Arab and Muslim writers as the "blessed land of the prophets and Islam's revered

leaders." The Mamluks revived Muslim sanctuaries that at-
tracted numerous pilgrims. In 1496, Mujir al-Din al-'Ulay-
mi authored The Glorious History of Jerusalem and Hebron, recounting Palestine's rich history.

The Ayyubid conquest and reassertion of Islam in Palestine significantly impacted the region's socio-religious
landscape. This era allowed for religious coexistence while
maintaining the Islamic identity of Palestine, marking a vital period in its ever-evolving history.

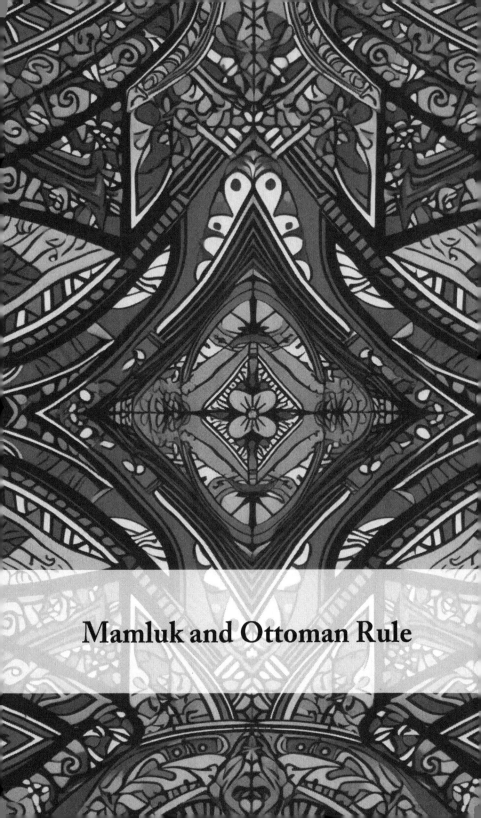

Mamluk and Ottoman Rule

Royal Pardon

Our journey in this chapter takes us to a time when two prominent empires – the Mamluks and the Ottomans – held sway over vast territories, wielding power and influence that reached far beyond their imperial borders. Their legacies not only cast a long shadow over the region they once ruled but also continue to impact the modern world in subtle yet significant ways.

The Mamluk Sultanate, which held control over Egypt, the Levant, and parts of the Arabian Peninsula, is a fascinating case study in social structure and governance. Born out of a military class of slaves and converts to Islam, the Mamluks created a stable and prosperous regime that lasted from 1250 to 1517. Their society was characterized by a distinctive social hierarchy, with the Mamluks occupying the ruling class and the remaining population falling under different categories of subjects. By analyzing the intricacies of Mamluk society and governance, we can gain insight into how a society established by a class of former slaves was able to survive and even thrive for centuries.

In 1517, the Ottoman Empire, under the leadership of Selim I, conquered the Mamluk Sultanate, ushering in a new era of rule in the region. As part of the Ottoman Empire, Egypt and its neighboring lands were exposed to an array of changes that ultimately shaped the political and social fabric we see today. The imperial administration introduced significant reforms, which aimed to centralize and rationalize the governance and taxation systems inherited from the Mamluks. The Tanzimat Reforms, which unfolded in the mid-19th century, were especially transformative, as they aimed to modernize the empire and strengthen its position in the rapidly changing global order.

As we delve deeper into this period of history, we shall also explore the role of the Ottoman Empire during the First World War and its collapse in the aftermath of the conflict. This tumultuous time brought about the end of a centuries-long rule over a diverse and interconnected world, setting the stage for future power dynamics in the region. Additionally, we will discuss the Balfour Declaration and its implications – how a single document has profoundly affected the lives of millions in the Middle East and is intertwined with the ongoing Israeli-Palestinian conflict.

Throughout this chapter, we shall endeavor to place these events, people, and ideas into their broader historical context. To understand why the Mamluk and Ottoman empires took the paths they did, we shall examine not only the facts of their history but also the underlying motivations, challenges, and ideas that propelled them forward. As we follow the destinies of these mighty empires and their legacies, we can derive valuable lessons about power, governance, and the ever-changing political landscape that continues to shape global events and human lives. By understanding the past, we gain a more profound appreciation for our world and the intricate tapestry of events, decisions, and consequences that underpins it.

Mamluk Rule and Social Structure

The rise of the Mamluk Sultanate can be traced back to the Ayyubid Dynasty, which was established by Salah al-Din, commonly known as Saladin, al-Ayyubi, in 1137. After successfully uniting the Muslim world under his rule, Salah al-Din managed to liberate Jerusalem and the surrounding areas from Crusader control. Under the Ayyubid rule, Palestine experienced a period of relative stability and prosperity that was interrupted by the frequent attacks by the Crusaders.

Eventually, the Ayyubid dynasty began to weaken due to internal power struggles and external threats. This provided an opportunity for the Mamluks, a military class made up of former slaves, to seize power. In 1260, the Mamluks were able to defeat the invading Mongols, and by 1291 they successfully expelled the remaining Crusader presence from Palestine. This marked the beginning of Mamluk rule over the region.

The social structure under the Mamluks was complex and hierarchical. At the top of the social pyramid were the sultans, followed by the Mamluk military elite, which came predominantly from enslaved populations in the Caucasus and Central Asia. The Mamluk military class held significant power and could even remove sultans if their interests were not represented. Beneath the military class were the local nobility and prominent families, who maintained their status through loyalty and service to the Mamluk administration.

The Palestinian peasantry formed the majority of the population and were divided into various categories, such as free peasants, tenant farmers, and sharecroppers. The peasantry played a critical role in the agricultural production of the region and, as such, held significant economic importance.

Under Mamluk rule, Palestine was divided into several administrative districts called wilayat, with major cities such as Jerusalem, Gaza, Ramla, and Hebron serving as the regional centers. The economy of Mamluk Palestine was primarily based on agriculture, as the fertile coastal plains, hilly landscapes, and the Jordan Valley provided excellent conditions for various crops, including grains, fruits, vegetables, and cotton. Trade also played an essential role in the economy, connecting Palestine to regional and international markets through vibrant commercial hubs like Acre and Damascus.

An emphasis on the construction of religious buildings and infrastructure projects, such as madrasas, mosques, hospices, bridges, and caravanserais characterized the Mamluk rule in Palestine. This period saw substantial advancements in Islamic culture, scholarship, and education due to the establishment of numerous educational institutions that fostered the study of Islamic theology, jurisprudence, and science. Despite being ruled by a Muslim majority, Palestine during the Mamluk era was marked by mutual coexistence and tolerance among diverse religious and ethnic groups, including Jews and Christians.

Towards the end of the Mamluk era, the sultanate experienced decline due to internal divisions, economic stagnation and vulnerability to external threats. The emergence of the powerful Ottoman Empire in the 15th century further weakened the Mamluk Sultanate.

The Mamluk period in Palestine is significant because it laid the foundations for the later socio-political and economic developments that would shape the region's history. The administrative systems, agricultural practices, and cultural advancements that emerged under Mamluk rule would be further developed during the Ottoman period. Connecting these events and themes with the subsequent historical periods in the book will help readers understand the long-lasting impact of Mamluk rule on the history of Palestine.

Ottoman Conquest

The struggle for control over Palestine began with hostilities between the Mamluks and the Ottoman Turks in 1486 as they battled for supremacy in western Asia. The Ottomans emerged victorious in 1516 at the Battle of Marj Dabiq, leading to their swift conquest of Palestine. During this conquest, they fought smaller engagements against the Mamluks in the Jordan Valley and at Khan Yunis on their way to the Egyptian capital. Additionally, minor uprisings occurred in Gaza, Ramla, and Safad, which the Ottomans quickly suppressed.

Upon their conquest of Palestine, the Ottomans maintained the existing Mamluk administrative and political structure. Greater Syria was established as an eyalet (province) ruled from Damascus. Within this eyalet, the Palestinian region was divided into five sanjaks, or provincial districts: Safad, Nablus, Jerusalem, Lajjun, and Gaza. These sanjaks were further divided into subdistricts called nawahi.

The Sublime Porte, the imperial government based in Istanbul, played a central role in the governance of Palestine during the 16th century. It was responsible for maintaining public order and domestic security, collecting taxes, regulating the economy, overseeing religious affairs, and ensuring social welfare. The majority of the Palestinian population, estimated to have been around 200,000 in the early years of Ottoman rule, lived in villages. The largest cities were Gaza, Safad, and Jerusalem, each containing between 5,000 and 6,000 residents.

The Ottomans' property administration comprised a system of fiefs called timar and trusts called waqf. Timar lands were given by the sultan to various officers and officials, mostly from the elite sipahi units. The holder of a timar land derived income from it while also being responsible for maintaining order and enforcing the law within its boundaries. Waqf lands were dedicated to religious functions, institutions, social welfare, and individual beneficiaries and were owned by various individuals. Significantly, over 60% of cultivated land in the Jerusalem Sanjak was waqf land. Private landownership also existed, primarily within villages and their immediate surroundings.

Although "Palestine" was no longer the official name of an administrative unit within the Ottoman Empire, the term persisted in popular and semi-official use. Examples of its usage from the 16th, 17th, and 18th centuries have survived, illustrating that the name remained recognized when referring to the region. Islamic jurists such as Sayf al-Islam Abu'l Sa'ud Effendi and Khayr al-Din al-Ramli offered differing interpretations of the term "Palestine." In European texts, such as Thomas Salmon's Modern history or, the present state of all nations, Jerusalem was still regarded as the capital city of Palestine, albeit in a diminished state from its ancient grandeur.

Tanzimat Reforms and their Effects

The Tanzimat reforms, initiated with the Gülhane Hatt-ı Şerif in 1839 and lasting until the First Constitutional Era in 1876, aimed to modernize and consolidate the social and political foundations of the Ottoman Empire. This era was characterized by various attempts to modernize the empire and secure its territorial integrity against both internal nationalist movements and external aggressive powers. The reforms sought to promote Ottomanism among the diverse ethnic groups of the empire and counter the rise of nationalism within its borders.

Historian Hans-Lukas Kieser argued that the Tanzimat reforms led to "the rhetorical promotion of equality of non-Muslims with Muslims on paper vs. the primacy of Muslims in practice." Other historians believe that non-Muslims' ability to assert their legal rights decreased during this period, which led to land seizures and emigration. A key aspect of the reform policy was an economic policy based on the Treaty of Balta Liman in 1838. While many changes improved civil liberties, some Muslims regarded these reforms as a foreign influence on the Islamic world, complicating the state's reformist efforts.

A series of constitutional reforms during the Tanzimat period led to significant changes in various areas of Ottoman society. The government established a modern conscripted army, reformed the banking system, decriminalized homosexuality, replaced religious law with secular law, and replaced traditional guilds with modern factories. Additionally, the Ottoman Ministry of Post was established in Constantinople (Istanbul) on 23 October 1840.

With the implementation of these reforms, the empire witnessed significant shifts in social, political, and economic dynamics. In Palestine, one can see the impact of the Tanzimat reforms on both the society and the economy. The transition from guild systems to modern factories altered traditional labor relationships and facilitated the growth of industries. Moreover, the economic policies derived from the Treaty of Balta Liman had far-reaching implications for trade, agriculture, and taxation systems in the region.

However, the Tanzimat reforms were not without controversy and opposition. Various factions within the empire, especially those Muslims who viewed the reforms as a threat to the Islamic world, pushed back against the changes. This resistance complicated the state's attempts at restructuring and modernization, highlighting the complexity of a diverse empire trying to balance tradition and progress.

By examining the Tanzimat reforms and their effects, we can gain a better understanding of the forces that shaped Palestine during this critical moment in history. Understanding the successes and challenges of the Tanzimat era helps to contextualize the progression of events in the region and the various influences that continue to shape it today.

World War I and the End of Ottoman Rule

The Ottoman Empire, at its zenith, was a vast multinational realm stretching from Eastern Europe to the Middle East and North Africa. However, by the early 20th century, it had been significantly weakened through a combination of internal strife and external pressure from European powers. As the shadow of World War I loomed ominously on the horizon, the Ottomans decided to ally with the German Empire and the Central Powers, hoping to secure military support to bolster their decaying empire.

This alliance suddenly placed the Ottoman Empire in direct conflict with the British Empire, which saw the opportunity to drive the Turks out of Palestine and other strategic territories. The British government sought to gain the support of the local Arab populations in these territories by engaging in secretive negotiations, in what would later become known as the Hussein-McMahon Correspondence (1915-16). In these negotiations, the British promised Sharif Hussein of Mecca, a leading Arab nationalist, that a united Arab state would emerge after the Ottoman Empire's defeat. This promise was instrumental in eliciting the Arab nations' support in the form of the Great Arab Revolt against the Turks during the war.

Parallel to these negotiations, the British and French governments secretly crafted the Sykes-Picot Agreement of 1916, which sought to establish a new balance of power in the Middle East by dividing Ottoman territories between themselves with little concerns for promises made to the various nationalist movements. This agreement directly contradicted the earlier promise made to Sharif Hussein, as it envisioned most of Palestine becoming an international zone under neither French nor British colonial control.

Adding to this complex web of duplicity, the British Foreign Secretary Arthur Balfour issued the Balfour Declaration in 1917, which pledged British support for creating a "Jewish national home" in Palestine. While seen as a momentous victory for Zionist aspirations, the declaration only intensified territorial competition and stoked animosity between the different nationalist factions.

On the battleground, the British-led Egyptian Expeditionary Force, commanded by General Edmund Allenby, proved to be too much for the beleaguered Ottoman Empire. Jerusalem fell to British forces on December 9, 1917, and by September 1918, Turkish forces in Palestine were utterly defeated at the Battle of Megiddo. By October 31, Turkey officially capitulated, marking the end of the Ottoman Empire's role in World War I.

The immediate aftermath of the war saw the fulfillment of the Sykes-Picot Agreement, as the region was indeed partitioned into British and French League of Nations mandates. However, the conflicting promises made to Arab nationalists and the Jewish population during the war led to a deep sense of betrayal among the people of Palestine and only served to sow the seeds of discord, setting the stage for the turbulent and tumultuous history that was to follow in the region.

The Balfour Declaration and its Implications

During World War I, the British government issued a public statement known as the Balfour Declaration, which declared its support for the establishment of a "national home for the Jewish people" in Palestine. This region, then under Ottoman rule, contained a minority Jewish population. The declaration was contained in a letter from the United Kingdom's Foreign Secretary Arthur Balfour to Lord Rothschild, a leader of the British Jewish community, who then transmitted it to the Zionist Federation of Great Britain and Ireland on November 2, 1917. The text of the declaration was published in the press on November 9, 1917.

Following the British declaration of war on the Ottoman Empire in November 1914, the British War Cabinet began discussing Palestine's future, with Zionist Cabinet member Herbert Samuel proposing support for Zionist ambitions to enlist Jewish backing in the wider conflict. In response, a committee was established by British Prime Minister H. H. Asquith in April 1915 to determine British policy towards the Ottoman Empire, including Palestine. Asquith, who had favored post-war reforms for the empire, resigned in December 1916 and was replaced by David Lloyd George, who favored partition.

The first negotiations between the British and the Zionists took place at a conference on February 7, 1917, including Sir Mark Sykes and the Zionist leadership. Further discussions resulted in Balfour's request on June 19 for Rothschild and Chaim Weizmann to submit a draft of a public declaration. The British Cabinet deliberated on subsequent drafts during September and October, incorporating input from Zionist and anti-Zionist Jews but excluding representation from the local population in Palestine.

By late 1917, the wider war had reached a stalemate: the United States had not yet suffered casualties, and the Russians were amidst a Bolshevik-led revolution. The Battle of Beersheba on October 31, 1917, broke a stalemate in southern Palestine, and the release of the final declaration was authorized the same day, reflecting the perceived propaganda benefits for the Allied war effort among the global Jewish community.

The Balfour Declaration represented the first public expression of support for Zionism by a major political power. The term "national home" had no international legal precedent and was intentionally vague regarding the contemplation of a Jewish state. The British government later confirmed that "in Palestine" meant that the Jewish national home was not intended to encompass the entirety of Palestine. The second half of the declaration addressed concerns that the policy would prejudice the local population's position and fuel global antisemitism. The declaration called for safeguarding the civil and religious rights of Palestinian Arabs, who composed the majority of the local population, and the rights and political status of Jewish communities in other countries.

The British government acknowledged in 1939 that the local population's views should have been considered and recognized in 2017 that the declaration should have called for the protection of Palestinians' political rights. The Balfour Declaration had far-reaching consequences, increasing popular support for Zionism within worldwide Jewish communities and becoming a central component of the British Mandate for Palestine—the founding document of Mandatory Palestine—and the ongoing Israeli-Palestinian conflict.

Although the declaration incited controversy over whether it contradicted earlier promises made to the Sharif of Mecca in the McMahon-Hussein correspondence, the Balfour Declaration and its implications continue to shape modern-day perspectives on the Israeli-Palestinian conflict.

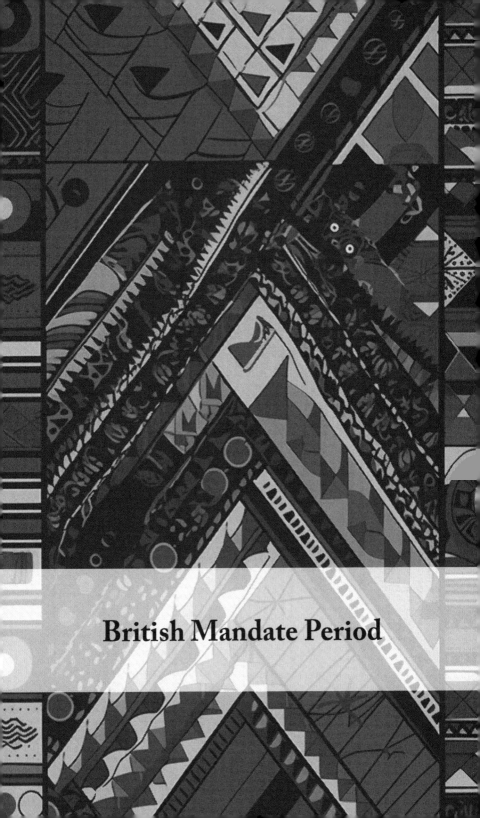

British Mandate Period

We will now discuss the period from the establishment of the British Mandate over Palestine, following the disintegration of the Ottoman Empire, to the conflicting promises made to the Jews and the Arabs. As we examine the implications of these unfolding events, we will witness the ensuing waves of Jewish immigration and the subsequent Arab revolts. This exciting narrative will engage us in the clashes of ideas, passions, and interests that colored this significant time.

As the Mandate period progressed, the tensions between the Zionist movement and the Arab population continued to escalate. The shadows of World War II loomed large, and the Jewish plight for survival grew even more desperate. Against this backdrop, the United Nations devised the Partition Plan, which attempted to resolve the competing national aspirations of the Jews and Arabs in the Mandate territory. As we delve into the intricacies and controversies of this landmark proposal, we will appreciate the multifaceted perspectives of the time and weigh the merits and demerits of the United Nations' endeavors.

Before we reach the end of the British Mandate period, we will chronicle the stirrings of war. In 1948, a cataclysmic conflict erupted, as neighbors, brothers, and friends took up arms against one another. The War of 1948 carved out new borders and birthed new nations, creating a distinctly new geopolitical tapestry. As history unfolded, the reverberations were felt across the globe, and the questions of identity, ancestry, and belonging continue to confront the people of Israel and Palestine even today.

Our exploration of the British Mandate period, with its

twists and turns, conflicts and compromises, hopes and losses, will enable us to draw connections and draw lessons from the past that remain relevant in our understanding of the present. We shall delve beneath the surface events, hungry to uncover the forces that propelled history forward and transformed this storied land. And as we read on, immersed in the rich tapestry of a bygone era, let us remember that the mark of any good history book lies in its ability to illuminate the past while shedding light on our present.

Establishment of the British Mandate

Mandatory Palestine was a geopolitical entity established between 1920 and 1948 in the region of Palestine under the terms of the League of Nations Mandate for Palestine. During the First World War, an Arab uprising against Ottoman rule and the British Empire's Egyptian Expeditionary Force drove the Ottoman Turks out of the Levant. The United Kingdom had agreed in the McMahon-Hussein Correspondence that it would honor Arab independence if the Arabs revolted against the Ottoman Turks, but in the end, the United Kingdom and France divided the area under the Sykes-Picot Agreement — an act of betrayal in the eyes of the Arabs.

Further complicating the issue was the Balfour Declaration of 1917, in which Britain promised its support for the establishment of a Jewish "national home" in Palestine. At the war's end, the British and French formed a joint "Occupied Enemy Territory Administration" in what had been Ottoman Syria. The British achieved legitimacy by obtaining a mandate from the League of Nations in June 1922. One objective of the League of Nations mandate system was to administer areas of the defunct Ottoman Empire "until such time as they are able to stand alone."

During the Mandate, the area saw successive waves of Jewish immigration and the rise of nationalist movements in both the Jewish and Arab communities. Following the arrival of the British, Arab inhabitants established Muslim-Christian Associations in all of the major towns. In

1919 they joined to hold the first Palestine Arab Congress in Jerusalem, aimed primarily at representative government and opposition to the Balfour Declaration. Concurrently, the Zionist Commission formed in March 1918 and became active in promoting Zionist objectives in Palestine.

In July 1920, a British civilian administration headed by a High Commissioner replaced the military administration. The first High Commissioner, Herbert Samuel, a Zionist and recent British cabinet minister, arrived in Palestine on 20 June 1920 to take up his appointment from 1 July. One of Samuel's first actions was to grant concessions from the Mandatory government over key economic assets. In 1921 the government granted Pinhas Rutenberg — a Jewish entrepreneur — concessions for the production and distribution of electrical power. Rutenberg soon established an electric company whose shareholders were Zionist organizations, investors, and philanthropists. Palestinian-Arabs saw it as proof that the British intended to favor Zionism.

Samuel tried to establish self-governing institutions in Palestine, as required by the mandate, but the Arab leadership refused to co-operate with any institution that included Jewish participation. When Grand Mufti of Jerusalem Kamil al-Husayni died in March 1921, High Commissioner Samuel appointed his half-brother Mohammad Amin al-Husseini to the position. Amin al-Husseini, who came from the al-Husayni clan of Jerusalem, was an Arab nationalist and Muslim leader. As Grand Mufti, al-Husseini played a key role in violent opposition to Zionism. In 1922, al-Husseini was elected President of the Supreme Muslim Council, which controlled the Waqf funds and the Islamic courts in Palestine.

The 1922 Palestine Order in Council established a Legislative Council, which was to consist of 23 members, but due to an Arab boycott of the elections, the results were annulled, and a 12-member Advisory Council was established. The area saw increased violence and unrest, such as the August 1929 riots, contributing to the eventual escalation into the Arab revolts and Jewish insurgency.

Zionist Immigration and Arab Revolts

During the British Mandate period, the Arab Revolt of 1936-1939 marked a significant turning point in the history of Palestine. Thousands of Palestinian Arabs were mobilized, fueling nationalistic sentiments through the Arabic press, schools, and literary circles. The catalyst for this revolt was the assassination of Sheikh Izz al-Dīn al-Qassām by the British in 1935 and the murder of two Jews in April 1936. As violence escalated, Qassāmite groups initiated general strikes in Jaffa and Nablus. Arab political parties then formed the Arab Higher Committee, led by the mufti of Jerusalem, Amīn al-usaynī, and demanded an end to Jewish immigration, a ban on land sales to Jews, and national independence.

With the support of neighboring Arab countries, the revolt became a large-scale national movement by the end of 1936, primarily driven by the Arab peasantry. However, the arrival of British troops in the region led to the deployment of firm measures against the uprising. In July 1937, the Peel Commission released its findings on the revolt, citing Arab desire for independence and fear of the Jewish national home as the main causes. The commission recommended partitioning Palestine, which was met with cautious acceptance by the Zionists but significant opposition from the Arabs, who were horrified by the idea.

Continuing violence and increasing unrest led to the British declaring martial law in September 1937, dissolving the Arab Higher Committee and arresting many of its members. The mufti of Jerusalem fled to Lebanon and from there to Iraq but continued coordinating the Arab Revolt until 1939. Despite the high casualty rates for the Arabs—more than 5,000 killed, 15,000 wounded, and 5,600 imprisoned—this revolt marked the birth of a national identity. The general strike, called off in October 1939, encouraged Zionist self-reliance, while the Arabs struggled to recover from their defiance against the British administration.

In response to the Peel Commission's recommendations, the Woodhead Commission was established to examine the practicality of partition. Finding the commission's plan unworkable, alternative proposals were put forth, limiting the area and sovereignty of the proposed states. Both Arabs and Jews found this unacceptable, leading to a round-table conference in London in 1939. However, no agreement was reached at the conference.

In May 1939, the British government issued the White Paper, which essentially yielded to Arab demands and marked the end of the Anglo-Zionist entente. While Arabs rejected the paper due to mistrust of the British government and opposition to certain provisions, the Zionists were left shocked and enraged by what they considered a death blow to their program. Nonetheless, significant progress had been made towards the establishment of a Jewish national home since 1918, setting the stage for the eventual creation of the State of Israel.

United Nations Partition Plan

On 29 November 1947, the United Nations General Assembly voted on Resolution 181 (II), recommending a partition plan with the Economic Union of Mandatory Palestine following the termination of the British Mandate. Although not legally binding, the plan called for the partition of Palestine into separate Arab and Jewish states and the establishment of a Special International Regime for the City of Jerusalem, which was to include Bethlehem. Zionist leaders, including the Jewish Agency, accepted this plan, while Palestinian Arab leaders vehemently rejected it. All independent Muslim and Arab states voted against the resolution.

The UN resolution on partition served as the catalyst for widespread sectarian violence, leading to a full-scale civil war. Hundreds of Arabs, Jews, and British citizens lost their lives in the hostilities that erupted over the following months. Amid ongoing Arab provocations and attacks, the Yishuv (Jewish community in Palestine) initially found itself on the defensive, while occasionally striking back against their aggressors. Arabs from the Arab Liberation Army entered Palestine to fight alongside indigenous Palestinians in the conflict.

However, the April–May offensive of Yishuv forces turned the tide in the conflict. Arab forces and Palestinian Arab society experienced a crushing defeat, with approximately 700,000 Palestinians displaced from their homes in the turmoil that followed. David Ben-Gurion, a prominent Zionist leader, declared the establishment of a Jewish state in Eretz Israel, to be known as the State of Israel, on 14 May

1948. This move prompted neighboring Arab states to intervene in an attempt to prevent the partition and support the Palestinian Arab population.

Transjordan and Egypt swiftly took control of territories designated for the future Arab State, while Syrian and Iraqi expeditionary forces unsuccessfully attacked the newly declared State of Israel. Jerusalem became the focal point for some of the most intense fighting, primarily between Jordanian and Israeli forces seeking to wrest control of the city. On 11 June, a truce was accepted by all parties to the conflict.

Israel seized the opportunity to reinforce its army during this ceasefire period. Its forces subsequently captured the whole of the Galilee region, as well as the Lydda, Ramle, and Negev areas in a series of military operations. Additionally, the Battles of Latrun led to securing a road linking Jerusalem to the rest of Israel. The war eventually ended with the signing of the 1949 Armistice Agreements by the neighboring Arab states, which also recognized, de facto, the new borders of Israel. During this phase, an additional 350,000 Arab Palestinians were displaced or expelled from areas conquered by Israel.

End of the War of 1948

In 1945, the Yalta Conference participants agreed arrangements for UN trusteeships over the existing League of Nations mandates, subsequently leading to significant developments in the Palestine Mandate. In response to the troubling conditions of the displaced persons camps in post-World War II Europe, described in the Harrison Report published in July 1945, British Foreign Secretary Bevin declared in October that Britain aimed to turn over its Palestine problem to the UN. However, he also stressed the need for Britain to first make efforts to resolve the situation to avoid accusations of evading its responsibilities.

By April 1946, the League of Nations had agreed to liquidate and transfer its assets to the UN. Meanwhile, its assembly showed support for the British intention to grant independence to Transjordan. Within the same month, the Anglo-American Committee of Inquiry published a report that steered further developments in Palestine. Subsequently, Transjordan legally gained independence in June 1946 with the ratification of the Treaty of London.

As the British struggled to address the Palestine issue, the Morrison-Grady Plan was proposed in July 1946 to implement Anglo-American recommendations. However, by 1947, the vehement disagreement between Britain and the United States during the London Conference on Palestine led to the outright rejection of both the Morrison-Grady and Bevin Plans by all involved parties. This prompted the British to refer the Palestine question to the UN in February 1947.

The United Nations Special Committee on Palestine (UN-SCOP) was established in May 1947 and published its report in September the same year. This culminated in the endorsement of the United Nations Partition Plan for Palestine in November 1947, calling for the end of the Mandate by August 1948 at the latest. Consequently, on 11 December 1947, Colonial Secretary Arthur Creech Jones announced that the British Mandate in Palestine would terminate on 15 May 1948.

To ensure the smooth transfer of responsibility over Palestine, the British requested that its question be placed on the General Assembly's agenda and called for a Special Session to form a committee for the issue's consideration. Although the five Arab UN member states' proposal on terminating the Mandate and declaring Palestine's independence was not accepted, the Ad Hoc Committee on the Palestinian Question was formed following the publication of the UNSCOP report in September 1947.

Prior to the end of the Mandate, the British had implemented regulations governing land transfers and issued immigration certificates to accommodate Jewish refugees in Europe. However, the new Labour Government, led by Clement Attlee and with Ernest Bevin as Foreign Secretary, decided to maintain the White Paper policy.

The 1947 UNSCOP resolution stoked the flames of conflict in Mandatory Palestine, as a civil war erupted between the Arab and Jewish communities. With the British Mandate nearing its end on 14 May 1948, the State of Israel was declared, and the Arab-Israeli War (1948) commenced. The British Cabinet decided in March 1948 that the civil and military authorities in Palestine should not oppose the establishment of the Jewish State nor any movement into Palestine from Transjordan.

Throughout these tumultuous times, Sir Henry Gurney filled the role of Chief Secretary in Palestine, recording events in his highly detailed and extensively annotated diary. His work serves as a testament to this critical and contested period in the history of Palestine, providing invaluable insight into the end of the British Mandate and the outbreak of the War of 1948.

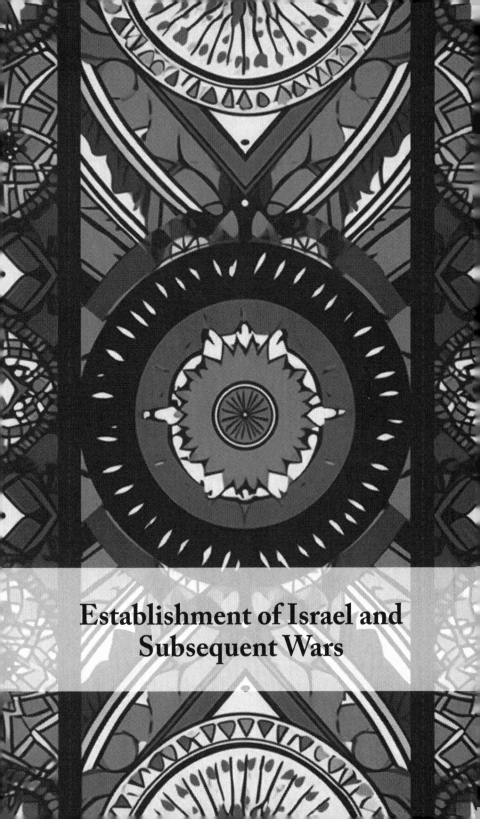

Establishment of Israel and Subsequent Wars

The establishment of the state of Israel in 1948 and the subsequent wars and crises that followed are a testament to the complex interweaving of religion, nationalism, and geopolitics in the shaping of the modern Middle East. In this chapter, we explore the events and people that played a crucial role in this transformative period, unraveling the multitude of factors that contributed to the region's seemingly endless cycle of violence and peacemaking.

We embark on this journey back in time, beginning with the founding of Israel and the ensuing displacement of the Palestinian people. As we examine this key turning point in history, we strive to present a balanced and objective perspective, taking into account the deeply held passion and conviction on both sides of the conflict, as well as the international community's involvement.

Moving forward, we delve into the Suez Crisis of 1956, an event that would uncover the deep-rooted animosities and insecurities that pitted nations against one another. It was during this time that the vestiges of colonial power began to crumble, and new alliances were forged, in a shifting landscape of international influence.

As we continue our narrative, we arrive at the fateful Six-Day War of 1967, a conflict that would irrevocably alter the geopolitical map of the Middle East, with repercussions that reverberate to this day. We explore the complex web of motivations and fears that led to the war, and the impact of its outcomes on regional and global politics at the time.

We then move on to the Yom Kippur War of 1973, a surprising and pivotal moment in the region's history that exposed the fragility of peace and the potential for sudden escalation. This was a time when allegiances and leadership would be put to the test, with consequences that still echo across the region.

Throughout this chapter, we will also examine the expansion of Israel's borders and the growth of settlements, delving into the political, ideological, and practical considerations that drove these events. By connecting these historical developments with current geopolitical realities, we shed light on the deeply ingrained tensions and deeply humanitarian issues that persist in the region today.

With each turn of the page, we invite you to accompany us on this journey through history, as we chronicle the complex and deeply emotional story that has shaped the modern Middle East. In our exploration, we will strive to piece together the intricate puzzle of motivations and consequences, weaving together a narrative as complex and multifaceted as the people who inhabited and continue to inhabit this ancient and storied land.

Founding of Israel and Displacement of Palestinians

In 1948, during the 1948 Palestine war, more than 700,000 Palestinian Arabs - about half of prewar Palestine's Arab population - were expelled or fled from their homes. This exodus marked a pivotal event in Palestinian society's fracturing, dispossession, and displacement, a period now known as the Nakba, or "catastrophe," in Arabic.

Between 400 and 600 Palestinian villages were destroyed, village wells were poisoned, and other sites were subject to the Hebraization of Palestinian place names. The precise number of refugees, many of whom settled in neighboring states, remains disputed, but around 80 percent of the Arab inhabitants of what became Israel left or were expelled from their homes. About 250,000-300,000 Palestinians fled or were expelled during the 1947-1948 civil war in Mandatory Palestine, before the Israeli Declaration of Independence in May 1948. This mass exodus was a key factor in the Arab League's decision to enter the conflict, sparking the 1948 Arab-Israeli War.

The causes of the Palestinian exodus are a subject of fundamental disagreement among historians. Factors contributing to the mass departure include:

1. Jewish military advances.

2. Destruction of Arab villages.

3. Psychological warfare and fear of another massacre by Zionist militias, especially after the controversial Deir Yassin massacre, which spurred many Palestinians to leave out

of panic.

4. Direct expulsion orders by Israeli authorities.

5. The demoralizing impact of wealthier classes fleeing.

6. A typhoid epidemic in some areas, attributed to Israeli well-poisoning.

7. Collapse in Palestinian leadership and Arab evacuation orders.

8. An unwillingness to live under Jewish control.

Following the events of 1948, a series of laws were passed by the first Israeli government that prevented Arabs who had left from returning to their homes or claiming their property. Consequently, many Palestinian refugees and their descendants remain in their host countries. Some have since described the expulsion of the Palestinians as ethnic cleansing, though others dispute this characterization.

The so-called Law of Return, which grants immigration and naturalization rights to any Jewish person and their family, allowing them to settle in Israel, is seen by some as evidence of apartheid practices against Palestinians, who have been denied the right of return. The status of Palestinian refugees, and whether Israel will allow them to return to their homes or provide compensation, remains a central issue in the ongoing Israeli-Palestinian conflict. To this day, the events of 1948 are commemorated by Palestinians on May 15, or Nakba Day, as a powerful reminder of their collective displacement and suffering.

The Suez Crisis of 1956

The nationalization of the Suez Canal Company by Egyptian President Gamal Abdel Nasser on July 26, 1956, marked a turning point in the relationships between Egypt, Britain, and France. Long wary of Nasser's intentions and his resistance to their political influence in the region, the British and French governments were incensed by his move, which followed months of escalating tensions. In response to this perceived threat to European colonial interests, the Eisenhower administration attempted to broker a diplomatic resolution to the dispute, fearing that military conflict between its NATO allies and Egypt could invite Soviet intervention.

U.S. Secretary of State John Foster Dulles proposed the creation of a Suez Canal Users' Association (SCUA), which aimed to give Britain, France, and Egypt equal stakes in the management of the canal. However, this and other U.S. and international mediation efforts failed to garner the full support of the parties involved. Amidst discussions with the United States from August to October, the British government repeatedly hinted at the possibility of using force against Nasser.

Simultaneously, British and French authorities conducted secret military consultations with Israel, which viewed Nasser as a threat to its security. These negotiations culminated in a joint plan to invade Egypt and overthrow Nasser. Israeli forces attacked across Egypt's Sinai Peninsula on October 29, 1956, quickly advancing to within 10 miles of the Suez Canal. Britain and France then deployed their own troops, ostensibly to protect the canal from the ongoing conflict between Israel and Egypt.

The Eisenhower administration, eager to distance the United States from European colonial actions and alarmed by the potential for Soviet involvement in the crisis, pressured Britain and France to accept a United Nations ceasefire on November 6. The United States also voted for U.N. resolutions that publicly condemned the invasion and approved the creation of a U.N. peacekeeping force. This public rebuke of two key allies led to temporary strains in relations between the United States, Britain, and France, contributing to the resignation of British Prime Minister Anthony Eden in January 1957.

Following the Suez Crisis, the Eisenhower administration established the Eisenhower Doctrine, which granted increased power to aid Middle Eastern countries as a means of countering Soviet influence in the region. Despite the initial diplomatic fallout, the U.S.–U.K. relationship ultimately recovered under the leadership of Eden's successor, Harold Macmillan, by March 1957.

Throughout the Suez Crisis, various parties grappled with conflicting interests, and efforts at mediation proved unsuccessful. The episode underscored the fragile balance of power in the Middle East, and the events of 1956 continue to inform contemporary regional dynamics. In examining the Suez Crisis, it remains vital to consider not only the actions of various governments but also the underlying intentions and motivations driving their decisions. By understanding these factors, historians can better appreciate the complex interplay between regional and global powers, as well as the long-term effects of this influential moment in history.

The Six-Day War of 1967

The Six-Day War, which took place from June 5 to June 10, 1967, was a brief but intense conflict between Israel and a coalition of Arab states, primarily Egypt, Syria, and Jordan. The conflict was set amid poor relations between Israel and its Arab neighbors following the 1949 Armistice Agreements, signed at the end of the First Arab-Israeli War. The heightened tensions between the two sides were further exacerbated in 1956 with the Suez Crisis when Israel invaded Egypt, which had blockaded the Straits of Tiran to Israeli shipping. This skirmish ultimately led to the re-opening of the Straits of Tiran and the deployment of the United Nations Emergency Force (UNEF) along the Egypt-Israel border.

In the months leading up to the Six-Day War, tensions continued to rise. Israel maintained that another Egyptian closure of the Straits of Tiran would be grounds for war. In response, Egyptian President Gamal Abdel Nasser announced in May 1967 that the Straits would indeed be closed to Israeli vessels. In preparation for a potential conflict, Nasser mobilized Egyptian forces along the border with Israel and ordered the withdrawal of UNEF personnel.

On June 5, 1967, as the UNEF was departing, Israel launched a series of preemptive airstrikes against Egyptian airfields and other military installations. Caught by surprise, Egypt's air forces were decimated, granting Israel air supremacy. In conjunction, the Israeli military began a ground offensive into Egypt's Sinai Peninsula and the Egyptian-occupied Gaza Strip. Despite initial resistance,

Nasser ultimately ordered the evacuation of Sinai, and by the sixth day of the conflict, Israel had taken control of the entire peninsula.

Jordan, which had entered into a defense pact with Egypt just a week before the war began, did not mount an all-out offensive campaign against Israel. However, it did launch attacks on Israeli forces to slow their advance. On the fifth day, Syria entered the fray, shelling Israeli positions in the north.

The war ended with ceasefires agreed upon between Egypt and Jordan on June 8, Syria on June 9, and finally signed with Israel on June 11. The conflict resulted in over 20,000 Arab casualties, while Israeli losses amounted to less than 1,000. In addition to combatant deaths, 20 Israeli civilians were killed in Arab air strikes on Jerusalem, 15 UN peacekeepers were killed by Israeli strikes in Sinai, and 34 US personnel were killed in the USS Liberty incident when Israeli forces attacked a US Navy technical research ship.

Upon the conclusion of the hostilities, Israel had seized the Golan Heights from Syria, the West Bank (including East Jerusalem) from Jordan, and the Sinai Peninsula and the Gaza Strip from Egypt. The Six-Day War had lasting consequences for the region, as approximately 280,000 to 325,000 Palestinians and 100,000 Syrians were displaced from the West Bank and Golan Heights, respectively. Nasser resigned in shame following Israel's victory but was later reinstated after a wave of protests in Egypt. The war's aftermath also led to the closing of the Suez Canal until 1975, significantly affecting oil deliveries from the Middle East to Europe via the canal and triggering the 1970s energy crisis and the 1973 oil crisis.

The Yom Kippur War of 1973

The Yom Kippur War, alternatively known as the Ramadan War or the October War, was a significant armed conflict that occurred from October 6 to 25, 1973. Israel faced a coalition of Arab states led by Egypt and Syria, with the majority of the fighting taking place in the Sinai Peninsula and the Golan Heights. These strategic territories had been captured by Israel during the previous Six-Day War of 1967. Egypt's primary objective was to seize the eastern bank of the Suez Canal, hoping to leverage these territorial gains to negotiate the return of the Israeli-occupied Sinai Peninsula.

The war began with a surprise attack by the Arab coalition on the Jewish holy day of Yom Kippur, which coincided with the tenth day of the Islamic holy month of Ramadan in that year. This attack caught Israel off guard, paving the way for initial advances by Egyptian and Syrian forces. In response to the outbreak of hostilities, both the United States and the Soviet Union provided massive resupply efforts to their respective allies, leading to a precarious encounter between the two nuclear-armed superpowers.

Fighting erupted when Egyptian and Syrian forces crossed their respective ceasefire lines with Israel, entering the Sinai Peninsula and the Golan Heights. Egyptian forces managed to cross the Suez Canal in Operation Badr and advanced into the Sinai Peninsula, while the Syrians coordinated an assault on the Golan Heights. Despite the initial successes, Israel managed to halt the Egyptian advance, causing a stalemate on that front. Simultaneously, Israeli forces pushed the Syrians back to the pre-war ceasefire lines and launched a counter-offensive deep into Syria.

Egyptian forces attempted to push further into the Sinai Peninsula but were unsuccessful, prompting Israeli forces to counter-attack by crossing the Suez Canal into Egypt and advancing towards Suez City. A series of ceasefires began on October 22, brokered by the United Nations, though they ultimately unraveled due to both sides accusing the other of breaches. Nonetheless, by October 24, Israel had successfully encircled the Egyptian Third Army and Suez City, bringing their forces within 100 kilometers of the Egyptian capital, Cairo. Tensions between the United States and the Soviet Union increased, resulting in a jointly enforced ceasefire on October 25, 1973, which officially ended the war.

In the aftermath of the Yom Kippur War, the psychological landscape of the region changed significantly. The Arab world, which had been previously humiliated by the Israeli victory in 1967, felt vindicated by their early successes in the conflict. Meanwhile, Israel realized that they could not always rely on their military prowess to dominate the Arab states. These changing dynamics played a crucial role in paving the way for the Israeli-Palestinian peace process.

The 1978 Camp David Accords, which emerged following the war, led to Israel returning the entire Sinai Peninsula to Egypt. Subsequently, the 1979 Egyptian-Israeli peace treaty marked the first instance of an Arab country recognizing Israel as a legitimate state. This development signaled Egypt's departure from the Soviet sphere of influence and the beginning of its realignment with the West.

In conclusion, the Yom Kippur War proved deeply influential in shaping the Middle East's political landscape and the relationships between the countries involved. While tensions remained, the conflict marked the beginning of a series of peace processes that would gradually change the dynamics of the region.

Israel's Expanding Borders and Settlements

Since the establishment of the State of Israel in 1948, its borders have been a subject of ongoing controversy. A significant turning point occurred in the aftermath of the Six-Day War in 1967, when Israel captured additional Arab territories, including the West Bank, Gaza Strip, Golan Heights, and the Sinai Peninsula. These expansions were met with mixed reactions from the international community, with some condemning the occupation while others advocating for negotiated settlement of the conflict.

While Israel returned the Sinai Peninsula to Egypt following the Camp David Accords in 1978, the situation for the West Bank and Gaza Strip evolved differently. Both areas saw the rapid expansion and construction of Israeli settlements. These early settlements laid the groundwork for Israel's central policies and strategies for expansion and establishment of settlements in these occupied territories.

There are several factors that motivated Israel to expand and establish settlements in these territories. Demographically, the Israeli government wished to solidify their presence in the West Bank by increasing the Jewish population. Economically, the acquisition of land could accommodate the increasing influx of Jewish immigrants from around the world, as well as offer potential for the development of agricultural, industrial, and tourism sectors. Additionally, securing borders and ensuring the security of the nation was paramount to Israel's government, further justifying their expansion and settlement policies.

Reactions to these settlements have been diverse. The Israeli government views them as integral to the security and continuity of the Israeli state. For Palestinians, these settlements represent a significant infringement on their right to self-determination and a violation of international law. UN resolutions, such as UN Security Council Resolution 242, have emphasized the "inadmissibility of the acquisition of territory by war", further complicating Israel's position. The international community has condemned settlement expansion as a violation of the Fourth Geneva Convention, which prohibits an occupying power from transferring its civilian population into the territory it occupies.

The expanding borders and settlements in the West Bank and Gaza Strip have further strained the already fraught peace process and hopes for a two-state solution. Settlements have resulted in a de facto annexation of territory and dislocation of Palestinian communities, sometimes through forced evictions and land confiscations. The expansion of settlements also had an impact on the environment, with the degradation of agricultural land and diminished resources.

Despite the Oslo Accords of the 90s, which provided the framework for a potential two-state solution, settlement expansion has continued into the present, with Israel constructing and expanding settlements deep into Palestinian territories. This situation remains a critical challenge for both regional and global peace initiatives, with both sides holding deeply entrenched and opposing positions.

Israel's expanding borders and settlements, especially in the West Bank and Gaza Strip, have been a complex and ongoing issue throughout its history. While various factors, such as demographic, economic, and security concerns, seem to have motivated the Israeli government to undertake such policies, the international community and Palestinians regard the settlements as occupying forces and illegal under international law. The issue of settlement expansion and Israeli borders remains a contentious and influential aspect of the history of Palestine and the prospects for peace in the region.

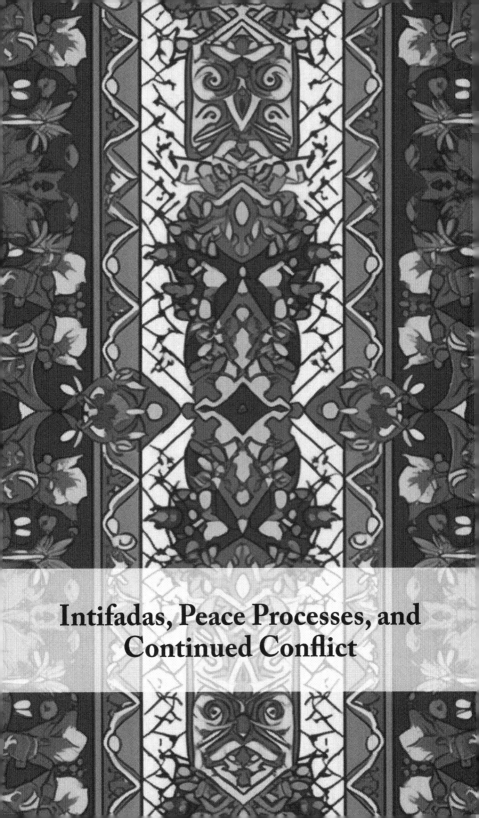

Intifadas, Peace Processes, and Continued Conflict

Lieutenant Maynard's Aftermath

In the years following the birth of the state of Israel and the resulting turmoil that engulfed the land, the quest for peace between Israelis and Palestinians began to take shape. The desire to bring an end to the seemingly endless cycle of violence and bloodshed has led to numerous attempts at reconciliation, with varying degrees of success. Caught in the middle of political maneuvering, diplomacy, and the aspirations of the two peoples involved, the history of the Israeli-Palestinian conflict has been marked by a series of significant events, which have indelibly shaped the region's present and future.

In this chapter, we shall embark on an exploration of the pivotal moments that have come to define the ongoing struggle for peace in the modern Israeli-Palestinian conflict. In narrating this historical arc, we shall spotlight the key characters— both Israelis and Palestinians— whose lives and decisions have shaped the trajectory of the conflict, delve deeper into the underlying themes, and examine the motives that have driven people to act. By presenting a balanced account of the various perspectives and controversies surrounding these events, we seek to provide readers with a comprehensive and objective understanding of this complex and ever-evolving conflict.

The First Intifada and the Oslo Accords represent one such period of immense significance. Sparked by years of frustration and resistance, the popular uprising of the First Intifada shattered the status quo and propelled both sides into a new world of diplomatic negotiations, culminating in the signing of the Oslo Accords. In examining this milestone, we shall scrutinize the successes and failures of these accords, how they influenced subsequent peace processes, and the lasting impression they left on the region.

The Second Intifada, however, would prove to be a markedly different chapter in the history of the conflict. The dynamics of violence and political upheaval during this period underscore the complexities of forging peace, as well as the fragility of coexistence between Israelis and Palestinians. We shall analyze the impact of the Second Intifada's violent events on the region's political landscape and the emergence of new players in the theater of conflict.

As the situation continued to evolve, another significant development would come in the form of Israel's disengagement from the Gaza Strip and the subsequent takeover by Hamas. In tracing these events and their consequences, we will seek to elucidate the shifting power dynamics and how they affect the prospect of peace in the region.

In the shadow of these momentous events, the search for peace has persisted, marked by various attempts to broker agreements and overcome obstacles to lasting reconciliation. We shall delve into the ins and outs of peace negotiations in the wake of the Second Intifada, as well as the trials and tribulations of the peace processes that continue to this day.

As the Israeli-Palestinian conflict persists, efforts to establish a sense of security and separation have generated significant controversy in the form of Israel's construction of the Separation Barrier. We will explore the Barrier's development and its impact on both Israelis and Palestinians, as well as the wider implications of its existence.

By exploring the interconnected web of events, motivations, and consequences that has shaped the modern Israeli-Palestinian conflict, we aim to provide an in-depth understanding of the context in which these struggles unfold and a window into the challenges that face those seeking peace. As history unfolds, the experiences of the past have the potential to inform new perspectives and approaches, offering valuable lessons for the future of this fraught and enduring conflict.

First Intifada and the Oslo Accords

The First Palestinian Intifada, a large-scale uprising against the Israeli occupation in the West Bank and Gaza Strip, erupted on December 9, 1987, and continued until 1993. The Intifada brought the Israeli-Palestinian conflict to international attention and laid the groundwork for the peace process that would follow.

The origins of the First Intifada can be traced back to multiple factors, including frustration with the continued Israeli occupation, socio-economic discontent, and the general sense of powerlessness experienced by the Palestinian population. The immediate spark that triggered the uprising was a traffic accident in the Gaza Strip, which led to the death of four Palestinians. Demonstrations quickly turned violent and spread throughout the occupied territories.

Palestinian tactics during the Intifada included protests, strikes, civil disobedience, and violence – ranging from stone-throwing to more lethal attacks on Israeli targets. The Israeli perspective on the unrest centered around national security concerns, and its response comprised a combination of military force and attempts to maintain control over the Palestinian population through curfews and other restrictions.

The First Intifada was marked by the involvement of various Palestinian factions, such as Fatah, Hamas, and the Popular Front for the Liberation of Palestine (PFLP), which united under the umbrella organization called the Unified National Leadership of the Uprising (UNLU).

136

These groups played key roles in coordinating and sustaining the rebellion.

By 1991, international pressure mounted for a peaceful resolution to the Israeli-Palestinian conflict, culminating in the Madrid Conference. The conference's goals were to establish a framework for negotiations between Israel and its Arab neighbors, as well as to initiate bilateral talks concerning the issues of territories, refugees, and the status of Jerusalem. The conference was attended by representatives from Israel, the United States, the Soviet Union, various Arab states, and a joint Palestinian-Jordanian delegation.

While the Madrid Conference did not yield immediate breakthroughs, it played a pivotal role in initiating the Israeli-Palestinian peace process. The secret negotiations that would eventually lead to the historic 1993 Oslo Peace Accords between the Palestinians and Israel took place in Norway, mediated by the Norwegian Foreign Ministry. The key negotiators for the Palestinians were Mahmoud Abbas and Ahmed Qurei from the Palestinian Liberation Organization (PLO), while the Israeli side was represented by Yossi Beilin and Shimon Peres.

The Oslo Accords, signed on September 13, 1993, sought to establish a framework for Palestinian autonomy in the West Bank and Gaza Strip and recognized the PLO as the legitimate representative of the Palestinian people. The Agreement also created the Palestinian Authority (PA), which would exercise limited self-rule in these areas over a five-year interim period.

The signing of the Oslo Accords was viewed optimistically by many as an opportunity for lasting peace in the region. However, the accords would ultimately fall short of their transformative potential due to a combination of factors, including the assassination of Israeli Prime Minister Yitzhak Rabin by a Jewish extremist, political changes in Israel, and continued violence and mistrust between Israelis and Palestinians.

In October 1994, Israel and Jordan signed a peace treaty – a significant development in the context of the First Intifada and the Oslo Accords. The treaty normalized relations between the two countries, resolving territorial disputes, and opening the door to economic cooperation. The Israel-Jordan peace treaty was an indicator that progress was possible in the region and offered hope for wider peace efforts.

In examining the First Intifada and the Oslo Accords, it is essential to acknowledge the different perspectives and experiences of both Israelis and Palestinians, while addressing the continuing controversies surrounding the conflict. The events of this period reveal the complexity and the difficulty of achieving peace in the Israeli-Palestinian conflict, even as they paved the way for subsequent peace processes and negotiations that continue to resonate in contemporary affairs.

Second Intifada and Political Changes

The Second Intifada, also known as the Al-Aqsa Intifada, began in late September 2000. Preceded by a period of on-and-off negotiations between Israel and Palestine, this uprising marked a violent shift in the dynamics of the conflict. The Al-Aqsa Intifada was characterized by Palestinian suicide bombings in Israel, which claimed the lives of many civilians, and Israeli military incursions into Palestinian territories, resulting in targeted killings of Palestinian militant leaders and organizers. The violence and bloodshed during this time strained the peace negotiation process and led to significant political changes in the region.

During the Al-Aqsa Intifada, Palestinian militants increased their attacks on Israeli civilians through the use of suicide bombings. In response to these attacks, the Israeli Security Forces launched full-fledged invasions into Palestinian civilian areas. In addition to taking a heavy toll on the civilian population, these invasions resulted in the destruction of infrastructure and widespread humanitarian crises.

Throughout the course of the Second Intifada, international actors played significant roles in mediating the conflict and proposing new resolutions. In 2002, the "Quartet" — a diplomatic group comprised of the United States, European Union, Russia, and United Nations — proposed the Road Map for Peace, a plan designed to resolve the Israeli-Palestinian conflict and lead to an independent Palestinian state living peacefully alongside Israel. In a historic speech on 24 June 2002, U.S. President George W. Bush became the first U.S. president to explicitly call for an independent Palestinian state, signaling a shift in American policy towards the conflict.

Amidst the escalating violence, Israel began constructing a complex security barrier in 2002, designed to prevent suicide bombers from crossing into the country from the West Bank. This barrier, which includes fences, rubble walls, and trenches, has been a source of controversy due to its negative impact on the lives and freedom of movement of the Palestinian population residing in the West Bank.

In an effort to reduce tensions and further pursue peace, Israel implemented the unilateral disengagement plan of 2004, withdrawing all settlers and most of its military presence from the Gaza Strip. Despite this pullout, Israel maintained control over Gaza's airspace and coastline, continuing its blockade and restrictions on the movement of people and goods in and out of the area. Additionally, in September 2005, Israel dismantled four settlements in the northern West Bank, further reinforcing its commitment to territorial concessions for peace.

These events, marked by violence and political changes, significantly impacted the negotiation process, and the consequences of the Second Intifada continue to shape contemporary perspectives on the Israeli-Palestinian conflict. Issues such as the Israeli Separation Barrier, the humanitarian crisis in the Gaza Strip, and the ongoing struggle for an independent Palestinian state remain at the forefront of the conflict today. The history of this tumultuous period provides valuable insights that are critical for understanding the ongoing complexities between Israel and Palestine and the challenges that lie ahead in the pursuit of lasting peace.

Gaza Disengagement and Hamas Takeover

The 2006 Palestinian legislative elections took place on January 25th, in a bid to elect the second Palestinian Legislative Council, the legislature of the Palestinian Authority (PA). Surprising both the international community and the Palestinian population, Hamas won a majority of the seats, securing 74 out of 132, while their rival, Fatah, won only 45. With this victory, Hamas was set to take control of most PA institutions.

Hamas attempted to form a unity government with Fatah, but their offer was rejected. In response to the election outcome, Israel and the United States imposed sanctions on the PA with the aim to destabilize the Palestinian government and provoke new elections. Although their efforts were ultimately unsuccessful in that regard, it significantly deepened the rift between Hamas and Fatah.

In June 2006, Palestinian militants affiliated with Hamas carried out a cross-border raid from Gaza into Israel through a tunnel dug for the purpose of attacking Israel. In this incursion, an Israeli soldier, Gilad Shalit, was captured and taken to Gaza by the militants. He would be held captive for five years until, in 2011, his captors released him in exchange for over 1,000 Palestinian prisoners who were being held in Israel. The abduction of Shalit prompted Israel to launch large-scale invasions of Gaza in the summer and autumn of 2006, in an attempt to rescue their missing soldier. Over 500 Palestinians and 11 Israelis lost their lives during these hostilities, but Israel was ultimately unsuccessful in retrieving Shalit.

Tensions between Hamas and Fatah continued to escalate as Palestinian President Mahmoud Abbas attempted to dismiss the Hamas-led coalition government in June 2007. Objecting to this move as illegal, Hamas members engaged Fatah members in street battles, which culminated in what became known as the 2007 Battle of Gaza. Victorious in their efforts, Hamas took control of the Gaza Strip.

From that point on, governance of the Palestinian territories has been divided between Hamas and Fatah. The European Union and several Western countries designate Hamas as an Islamist terror organization. Hamas now controls the Gaza Strip, while Fatah maintains authority over the West Bank.

As of July 2009, approximately 305,000 Israelis lived in 121 settlements in the West Bank, while an estimated 2.4 million West Bank Palestinians (according to Palestinian evaluations) lived primarily in four blocs centered in Hebron, Ramallah, Nablus, and Jericho.

The Gaza Disengagement and Hamas Takeover have significantly shaped present-day Israeli-Palestinian conflict dynamics. The division in Palestinian governance alongside an escalating humanitarian crisis in Gaza further complicates the already fraught situation. Understanding this context is essential in gaining a comprehensive perspective on ongoing peace processes and the obstacles that must be overcome to achieve viable solutions for both Israelis and Palestinians.

Continued Peace Processes and Obstacles

Following the Oslo Accords, various summits, conferences, and diplomatic efforts have been undertaken to bring a peaceful resolution to the Israeli-Palestinian conflict. One of the most significant attempts was the Camp David Summit in 2000, where U.S. President Bill Clinton brought together Israeli Prime Minister Ehud Barak and Palestinian leader Yasser Arafat. The talks aimed at reaching an agreement to end the longstanding conflict and address crucial issues such as borders, security, Palestinian refugees, and the status of Jerusalem. Despite high hopes, the Camp David Summit resulted in an impasse, with both sides unable to overcome their differing positions on critical issues.

In the wake of the failure at Camp David, the peace process saw renewed efforts with the introduction of the Roadmap for Peace in 2003, presented by the United States, Russia, the European Union, and the United Nations (the Quartet). The initiative called for a two-state solution with the establishment of an independent Palestinian state by 2005, based on a series of reciprocal steps by both Israelis and Palestinians. However, with both sides failing to uphold their commitments and violence continuing to escalate, the Roadmap for Peace did not attain the desired outcome.

The Annapolis Conference in 2007 marked another significant effort to broker a peace deal. The conference, led by the U.S. Bush administration, convened Israeli Prime Minister Ehud Olmert, Palestinian President Mahmoud Abbas, and representatives from over 40 nations. Despite high hopes and a joint statement pledging to undertake continuous, good-faith negotiations, the Annapolis Conference could not produce a lasting resolution to the conflict.

Throughout these peace initiatives, several obstacles have hindered the progress toward a peaceful resolution. Mutual distrust between Israelis and Palestinians persists, fueled in part by acts of violence committed by both sides. Moreover, internal political divisions within the Israeli and Palestinian societies complicate the negotiations, with different factions pursuing divergent agendas. Additionally, external actors such as the United States, United Nations, Egypt, and Jordan have at times played a role in the peace processes in ways that affect the outcomes.

Influential leaders and negotiators, such as Yasser Arafat, Mahmoud Abbas, Ehud Barak, Ariel Sharon, Ehud Olmert, Benjamin Netanyahu, and key U.S. diplomats, have all played roles in shaping the peace processes. Their efforts to facilitate negotiations and navigate the complex political landscape have undoubtedly influenced the dynamics of the Israeli-Palestinian conflict. However, achieving a consensus on core issues has proven to be an elusive goal. The lack of agreement on borders, security, Palestinian refugees, the status of Jerusalem, and the establishment of a Palestinian state continues to challenge peace efforts.

It is essential to approach the ongoing search for a peaceful resolution with objectivity and fairness in presenting historical facts and events. The complexities surrounding the peace processes require a balanced analysis that acknowledges the different perspectives and legitimate grievances of each side. By doing so, this section will paint a comprehensive and engaging picture of the continued peace processes and obstacles in the Israeli-Palestinian conflict, providing readers with a deeper understanding of this enduring issue.

In conclusion, understanding the past failures and successes in the peace processes provides insights into current dynamics and potential paths forward. While lasting peace remains elusive, it is crucial to continue examining the ongoing attempts to secure a resolution to the Israeli-Palestinian conflict and the barriers that obstruct progress.

The Israeli Separation Barrier and its Impact

The construction of the Israeli Separation Barrier, also known as the Wall or the Security Fence, dates back to the early 2000s when a decision reflected Israel's deep concern over escalating terrorist attacks emanating from the West Bank. The barrier's primary stated objective by Israel was the prevention of terrorism and ensuring the security of its citizens. However, its significance has been highly contested, as Palestinians and international organizations argue that its route and construction serve as tools for the annexation of Palestinian land and the restriction of Palestinian movement.

The construction of the barrier began in 2002, during a period of intense violence associated with the Second Intifada. Its presence instantly provoked strong international and regional reactions, with strong opposition mainly focused on its route that in some stretches extends deeply into the West Bank, cutting off Palestinian communities from their livelihoods, schools, healthcare facilities, and agricultural lands.

For the Palestinians, the barrier has had profound effects on day-to-day life. Many who live close to it experience severe limitations on their freedom of movement, making commuting to workplaces, schools, and hospitals, no longer a simple task. This restriction has disproportionally hindered economic opportunities, access to education, and healthcare for the Palestinians. Additionally, the barrier has split families and communities apart, forcing many to make difficult choices about where and how to live.

The Palestinian agriculture sector, in particular, has suffered significant consequences. Farmers who have had their lands isolated by the barrier have struggled to access it due to stringent permit restrictions. As a result, crop yields have dwindled, and many have been forced to abandon their agricultural pursuits altogether. Environmental concerns have also arisen from the construction of the barrier, such as deforestation and soil erosion, further exacerbating the region's already fragile ecosystem.

On the other hand, the Israeli narrative surrounding the barrier is predominantly centered on security. Since its construction, there has been a significant reduction in the number of terrorism-related incidents and fatalities in Israel, contributing to a heightened sense of safety within the country. Nevertheless, the economic and social consequences faced by Israeli settlers living beyond the barrier have also surfaced, as they often face difficulties traveling and accessing services in Israel proper.

The legality of the Israeli Separation Barrier has been a matter of international scrutiny and heated debate. In 2004, the International Court of Justice issued an advisory opinion declaring the construction of the barrier to be illegal under international law and called for its dismantlement. Additionally, several United Nations resolutions have condemned its construction, citing violations of human rights and the detrimental implications for the peace process.

The long-term implications of the Israeli Separation Barrier on the resolution of the Israeli-Palestinian conflict are significant and multifaceted. Its existence has undoubtedly affected the prospects for a two-state solution by altering the physical realities on the ground and further complicating the negotiations between Israel and Palestine. Moreover, the psychological and emotional scars left by the barrier have deepened feelings of mistrust and hostility between the two communities, further widening the chasm that any peace process must bridge.

In this section of The History of Palestine, the Israeli Separation Barrier's multifaceted impact has been analyzed, ranging from individual stories to international viewpoints. By embracing a comprehensive and balanced approach to understanding its origins, consequences, and controversies, a clearer picture of the barriers' role within the larger historical narrative can be appreciated. As the history of Palestine continues to unfold, the Israeli Separation Barrier will undoubtedly remain a critical and contentious issue that shapes the prospects for peace and reconciliation in the region.

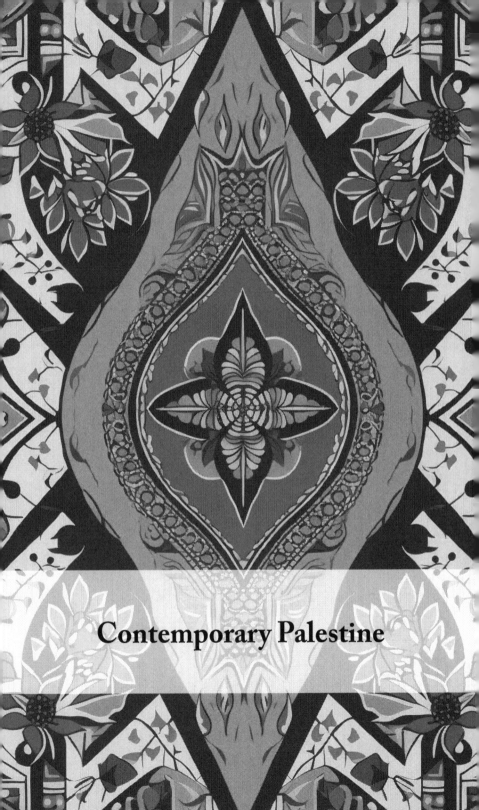

Contemporary Palestine

Contemporary Palestine is a land rich in history, immersed in countless layers of complexity and contradictions. To understand its present, one must look to the distant and more recent past, peering into the different periods, influences, and events that have continuously remolded it. As the reader embarks on this journey through the annals of Palestinian history and the intricacies of its modern-day challenges, it becomes evident that its struggles are not only rooted in the events of the previous century but are also interwoven with the contemporary issues it faces today.

At first glance, the ongoing tensions between Fatah and Hamas shed light on the political and ideological rifts within Palestinian society, reflecting deeper issues that have impeded the realization of a unified and independent nation. The historical backdrop, animosities, and subsequent rivalries between these factions will soon be explored, offering valuable insights into the nature of their divides and influences on the broader Palestinian context.

The city of Jerusalem, sacred and coveted by various communities and religions, remains at the heart of the Israeli-Palestinian conflict. Throughout the years, its symbolic significance, disputed status, and the diverse perspectives it engenders continue to kindle impassioned debates and bolster the uncertainty around its future. As this narrative leads the reader throughout the chronicles of this city, it will unearth the sensitivities, the roots of contention, and the potential bearing on prospects for peace.

Similarly, the realities of life in the Occupied Territories call for a deeper understanding of the conditions and constraints faced by Palestinians under an enduring military occupation. By shedding light on the interplay of human, political, and economic factors that have shaped their existence, we can better comprehend the struggles they endure and examine the ways in which their quality of life and aspirations for the future are influenced.

In the midst of these themes, the role of international organizations has taken on particular prominence in shaping both the political dynamic between Israel and Palestine and the discourse surrounding human rights and international law. As we delve into the intricacies of Palestinian statehood, the involvement of these organizations – their successes, failures, and limitations – serves as a reminder that the wider international community plays a significant role in resolving or exacerbating conflicts.

Finally, the ultimate aim of this historiographical endeavor is to tackle the most elusive and challenging question of all: What does the future hold for the Palestinian people and their quest for statehood? By providing objective analysis and exploring the feasibility of different scenarios, including a two-state solution and sustained struggles for peace, this effort at understanding the forces that shape contemporary Palestine will strive to illuminate potential pathways toward harmony and coexistence.

The Role of International Organizations

The United Nations (UN) has arguably been the most prominent international organization involved in Palestinian affairs since the establishment of Israel in 1948. In 1947, the United Nations General Assembly passed Resolution 181, which called for the partition of Palestine into separate Jewish and Arab states, with an internationalized Jerusalem. Following the 1948 Israeli War of Independence, the UN established the United Nations Relief and Works Agency for Palestine Refugees in the Near East (UNRWA) to assist Palestinian refugees who were displaced as a result of the conflict.

Over the years, the UN has passed numerous resolutions pertaining to Palestine, most notably in the context of the Israeli-Palestinian conflict. These resolutions have addressed issues such as Israeli settlements, Palestinian statehood, and the status of Jerusalem. For instance, UN Security Council Resolution 242, passed in 1967, called for Israel to withdraw from the territories it occupied during the Six-Day War and affirmed the right of every state in the region to live in peace and security. Additionally, in 2012, the United Nations General Assembly voted to upgrade the status of Palestine to a non-member observer state, a move seen as a symbolic recognition of Palestinian statehood.

The European Union (EU) has also played a significant role in Palestine, providing financial aid, diplomatic support, and technical assistance. The EU has been the largest donor of financial assistance to the Palestinian territories, contributing to vital sectors such as education, health, and infrastructure. The EU has also taken a more assertive diplomatic role in recent years, calling for an end to Israeli settlement expansion and advocating for a negotiated two-state solution based on the 1967 borders.

The Arab League, a regional organization comprising 22 Arab countries, has been an important advocate for Palestinian rights and interests. In 2002, the Arab League proposed the Arab Peace Initiative, which offered normalization of relations between the Arab countries and Israel in exchange for Israel's withdrawal from occupied territories and the establishment of a sovereign, independent Palestinian state. Although the initiative has not been fully implemented, it remains a reference point in the peace process.

In examining the impact of these organizations on contemporary Palestine, it is important to acknowledge their successes and challenges. For instance, UNRWA has provided crucial humanitarian assistance to millions of Palestinian refugees, ensuring access to education, healthcare, and relief services. However, the organization has faced funding shortfalls, political controversies, and accusations of having perpetuated the refugee issue rather than resolved it.

Moreover, critics argue that international organizations have not been able to bring about lasting peace or substantive progress in the Israeli-Palestinian conflict, despite numerous attempts. They point to the ongoing occupation, expanding settlements, and escalating tensions as indications that these organizations have fallen short of their goals.

On the other hand, proponents argue that international organizations play a vital role in providing humanitarian aid, fostering international awareness, and maintaining the possibility of a negotiated peace. They highlight the importance of international organizations' support for Palestinian state-building and their efforts in holding the parties accountable for violations of international law.

In the quest for peace and statehood, international organizations have played varied roles, from hosting peace negotiations, such as those at Camp David and Annapolis, to funding development projects aimed at improving life for Palestinians. As the landscape continues to evolve, these organizations may find opportunities to play constructive roles in mediating between the parties, addressing pressing humanitarian concerns, and fostering an environment conducive to peace.

Palestinian Political Divisions: Fatah and Hamas

In order to understand the contemporary Palestinian political divisions, it is essential to examine the two major factions competing for influence and control over Palestinian territories: Fatah and Hamas. Both organizations have played a pivotal role in shaping the political landscape of Palestine and have greatly influenced the Israeli-Palestinian conflict.

Fatah, the older of the two factions, was founded in the late 1950s by a group of leaders, including the iconic figure Yasser Arafat. Emerging from the Arab nationalist movement, Fatah's main goal was to establish a Palestinian state in the territories occupied by Israel after the 1967 Six-Day War. For decades, Fatah served as the backbone of the Palestine Liberation Organization (PLO), representing the broader Palestinian cause in the international arena and leading various armed resistance efforts against Israeli occupation. Gradually, Fatah shifted from its initial revolutionary principles, and after the Oslo Accords in 1993, it became the dominant political force in the Palestinian Authority (PA), responsible for administering the West Bank.

Hamas, on the other hand, originated from a different ideological background. Founded in 1987 as an offshoot of the Muslim Brotherhood, Hamas (an acronym for "Islamic Resistance Movement") sought to merge Palestinian nationalism with Islamic principles. It gained significant support within the Palestinian territories for its grassroots social services and dedication to armed resistance against

Israeli occupation. Over the years, Hamas grew in strength and became recognized as a leading force in the Palestinian political arena.

The ideological and strategic differences between Fatah and Hamas have led to a complex relationship marked by both collaboration and rivalry. During the First Palestinian Intifada (1987–1993), the factions cooperated against the common Israeli foe. However, as Fatah gravitated towards diplomacy and negotiations with Israel, Hamas adhered to armed resistance as the primary means for achieving Palestinian statehood, deepening the divide between the two organizations.

This division culminated in the 2006 Palestinian legislative elections when Hamas won a majority of seats in the Palestinian Legislative Council, unseating Fatah as the dominant political force. The electoral victory led to a power-sharing agreement between the two factions, but it quickly unraveled, leading to a brief but violent conflict in Gaza in 2007. Ultimately, Hamas expelled Fatah from the territory, establishing complete control over the Gaza Strip. Since then, the West Bank (administered by Fatah) and the Gaza Strip (controlled by Hamas) have been ruled separately, with little prospect for reconciliation.

The repercussions of this division on the Palestinian territories have been profound. The political split has limited the ability of the Palestinian leadership to present a united front in negotiations with Israel and to address the ever-growing challenges faced by Palestinians living under occupation. Furthermore, the situation in Gaza has been further exacerbated by the ongoing Israeli blockade and multiple military operations launched by Israel against Hamas, resulting in humanitarian crises in the densely populated area. The division also played into the hands of Israeli government hardliners who argue that no negotiated settlement is possible as long as Palestinian factions remain divided and at odds with each other.

In conclusion, the political divide between Fatah and Hamas has had a substantial impact on the Palestinians' pursuit of statehood and self-determination. Both factions must find ways to put aside their differences and commit to a unified and cohesive strategy in their struggle for independence. The potential for reconciliation remains uncertain, but it is a crucial component for the future of the Palestinian territories and the broader search for peace in the region.

As the Palestinian political landscape moves forward, both Fatah and Hamas will continue to play crucial roles in shaping the prospects for a just and lasting resolution to the Israeli-Palestinian conflict. Their actions will not only determine the future of the Palestinian people but will also have significant implications for regional stability, international relations, and the global fight for peace and justice.

The Status of Jerusalem

Jerusalem holds great significance for the three Abrahamic religions—Judaism, Christianity, and Islam. It is home to key religious sites, such as the Western Wall, the Church of the Holy Sepulcher, and Al-Aqsa Mosque. Consequently, the city has been a focal point of political and territorial disputes throughout history and remains at the heart of the Israeli-Palestinian conflict.

Following the creation of the State of Israel in 1948, Jerusalem was divided into West Jerusalem, controlled by Israel, and East Jerusalem, under Jordanian administration. The 1967 Six-Day War resulted in a significant shift, as Israel captured East Jerusalem and later annexed it, in a move not recognized by the international community.

The Israeli annexation of East Jerusalem has sparked controversy and remains a contentious issue. Israel claims a united Jerusalem as its capital, while Palestinians view East Jerusalem as the capital of a future Palestinian state. The international community has, by and large, refrained from recognizing Israeli sovereignty over East Jerusalem. However, some countries, notably the United States, have made moves to acknowledge Jerusalem as Israel's capital, further complicating the situation.

Recent developments, such as the United States' decision to move its embassy from Tel Aviv to Jerusalem in 2018, have added to the controversy surrounding the city's status. The move was met with widespread criticism from the international community and protests from Palestinians, as it was seen as an endorsement of Israel's claim over the entire city. This decision has significant implications for the future status of Jerusalem and the prospects for a peace agreement between Israel and Palestine.

The impact of the Jerusalem issue on the daily lives of its residents cannot be understated. Demographics have shifted over time, with Israeli settlement expansion in East Jerusalem contributing to tensions between Israeli and Palestinian communities. Freedom of movement, particularly for Palestinians in East Jerusalem, is restricted due to the security measures in place. Israeli control also affects access to religious sites, creating additional friction between groups.

Several proposals have sought to resolve the status of Jerusalem, such as shared sovereignty or a two-capital arrangement, with Israel maintaining control over West Jerusalem and Palestinians establishing East Jerusalem as their capital. A mutually agreed-upon resolution is essential for any progress to be made in reaching a comprehensive peace agreement between Israel and Palestine.

The status of Jerusalem remains a crucial component of contemporary Israeli-Palestinian issues. The city serves as a symbol of national aspirations for both Israelis and Palestinians and will continue to shape the future of peace and statehood for both parties. As such, the resolution of Jerusalem's status will be instrumental in determining how the broader conflict unfolds in the years to come.

Life in the Occupied Territories

Today, the lives of the more than five million Palestinian residents in the occupied territories are shaped by myriad factors, including the ongoing Israeli security measures, the restrictions on movement, economic difficulties, and internal divisions among Palestinians themselves. The following narratives help paint a portrait of the daily struggles and resilience of Palestinians living under occupation.

The 1993 Oslo Accords, intended to be a stepping stone toward a finalized peace agreement, established the temporary division of the West Bank into areas A, B, and C. Unfortunately, this arrangement remains in place to this day, contributing to a fragmented territory, restricted movement, and limited autonomy for region's Palestinian inhabitants. The landscape is peppered with Israeli settlements – a highly contentious issue – which have been deemed illegal by international law and create a constant source of tension.

An emblematic example of the daily struggles faced by Palestinians is the tense relationship between the Palestinian village of Yanoun, located in Area B, and the neighboring Israeli settlement of Itamar in Area C. Residents of Yanoun must navigate the friction between the two communities, including hostility from some Itamar settlers and restrictions on movement and land use. At the same time, the Palestinian villagers persist in their efforts to maintain their ancestral land and maintain peaceful relations with their neighbors.

In the Gaza Strip, conditions are markedly different and

arguably more dire. The region has been under a severe Israeli-led blockade since 2007, following the electoral victory of the Islamist group Hamas. This has led to a profound humanitarian crisis, with critical shortages in basic necessities like water, electricity, and sanitation, as well as sufficient healthcare access. The United Nations has warned that Gaza could become unlivable by 2020 if significant improvements are not made in these sectors.

One Gazan, Dr. Tarek Loubani, has spent years in the strip as an emergency room doctor, bearing firsthand witness to the harrowing medical conditions faced by his patients and colleagues alike. Severe shortages of supplies, combined with outdated facilities and insufficient training, have forced doctors like Loubani to innovate under desperate circumstances. Loubani's own determination and bravery, as well as his plight to save lives amid crushing odds, is a testament to the spirit of resilience exhibited by many Palestinians in the occupied territories.

While many Palestinians in the occupied territories grapple with poverty and unemployment, various initiatives have been created to foster economic development and sustainable livelihoods in spite of the challenges. One of these initiatives, the Canaan Fair Trade cooperative, has established the world's largest organic olive grove in the village of Burqin, located in the West Bank. The project provides a crucial source of income for thousands of farmers, as well as a sense of dignity that transcends the restrictions of occupation.

Despite the harsh conditions, many Palestinians have held on to their culture and identity, using them as sources of strength and resilience. One prominent example is the Freedom Theatre, a playhouse in the Jenin refugee camp. Founded by Juliano Mer-Khamis, the son of an Israeli father and a Palestinian mother, the theater has helped inspire and empower local youth through self-expression, often addressing the realities of occupation and steady undercurrent of violence they face.

These are just a few snapshots of life in the occupied Palestinian territories, and the resilience of its people. Such stories illustrate that amid the day-to-day hardships, there are also glimmers of hope in the form of cooperation, creativity, and determination. Whether it be the spirit of Yanoun's villagers, Dr. Loubani's life-saving work, the hope provided by initiatives like Canaan Fair Trade, or the healing power of theater in Jenin, these narratives serve as both a testament to Palestinian endurance and an important reminder of the human side of a deeply entrenched geopolitical dispute.

Future Prospects for Peace and Statehood

Over the past few decades, various peace initiatives have been proposed and pursued to resolve the Israeli-Palestinian conflict. The Oslo Accords, signed in 1993, marked a significant step towards establishing a Palestinian state. The agreements facilitated coordination between Israel and the Palestine Liberation Organization (PLO) on issues such as security, water, and borders. However, the Oslo process stalled due to numerous factors, including political instability, continued settlement expansion by Israel, and violence from both sides.

Another prominent peace effort was the Camp David Summit in 2000, which aimed to resolve the final status issues such as Jerusalem, borders, and refugees. The summit failed due to disagreements over the specifics and mistrust between the parties. The aftermath of the summit saw the eruption of the Second Intifada, a violent uprising, further complicating the peace efforts.

Key players in the peace process include the Palestinians and Israelis, as well as the international community. The Palestinian factions involved are primarily Fatah, which controls the Palestinian Authority (PA) in the West Bank, and Hamas, governing the Gaza Strip. For the Israelis, there has been a shift from moderate governments and parties to more right-wing positions, impacting the peace process negatively. The international community, including the United States, European Union, United Nations, and Arab League, have played crucial roles in peace negotiations and as mediators. However, varying geopolitical interests, regional competition, and changes in global leadership often impact the efficacy of the international community's involvement.

Public opinion on the prospects for peace varies between Palestinians and Israelis and has evolved over time. Factors such as political changes, economic crises, social media messaging, and regional developments have influenced opinions. For example, following the Arab Spring, the blurring of traditional alliances and the emergence of new regional conflicts shifted the focus away from the Israeli-Palestinian conflict. Additionally, normalization of relations between Israel and several Arab countries led a portion of Israelis to believe peace with Arab countries is more achievable than a resolution with the Palestinians.

Various scenarios have been proposed for the future of Palestine. The two-state solution remains the most widely supported, though increasing challenges, such as ongoing Israeli settlement expansion, impact the viability of this solution. An alternative one-state solution envisions a single democratic state for both Israelis and Palestinians, yet questions of national identity, security, and political representation complicate this approach. Other proposals, such as a confederation between Israel, Jordan, and Palestine, or provisional arrangements for Palestinian statehood, have also been suggested.

The unresolved conflict not only affects the everyday lives of people in the occupied territories but also has implications for regional and global stability. Issues such as economic deprivation, restricted movement, and lack of political autonomy are critical for those living within the West Bank and Gaza Strip. The international community grapples with the ongoing humanitarian crisis in Gaza, and any escalation of violence in Gaza, the West Bank, or Israel influences regional politics.

In conclusion, the prospects for peace and statehood in contemporary Palestine remain uncertain. However, understanding historical and current initiatives and complexities aids in predicting possible future scenarios. The resolution of the conflict will require genuine efforts by all parties involved, including addressing the root causes and confronting past failures. Meanwhile, it is essential to continue examining the impact of this unresolved conflict on the lives of those who experience it daily and the wider region.

Thank you!

We greatly value your feedback on this book and invite you to share your thoughts with us. As a growing independent publishing company, we are constantly striving to enhance the quality of our publications.

To make it easy for you to provide your insights, the QR code located to the right will directly lead you to the Amazon review page, where you can share your experience and offer any suggestions for improvement that you may have.

Related books

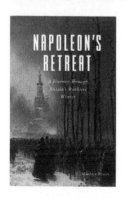 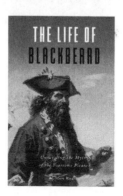 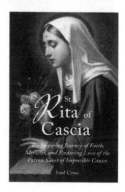

Scan the QR code below to browse our selection of related books and access exclusive supplemental materials:

Printed in Great Britain
by Amazon

31327714R00095